KEYS TO THE KINGDOM

Principles at Work in the Spiritual World

William S. McBirnie

HOUSE

LAKE MARY, FL 32746

Creation House
Strang Communications Company
600 Rinehart Road
Lake Mary, FL 32746
(407) 333-0600

Unless otherwise noted, all Scripture quotations are from
the King James Version of the Bible.

CONTENTS

Part 3: Our Destiny in Christ

I have read Dr. McBirnie's books and publications over a period of more than thirty years and have always been impressed with their sound doctrine, clarity of thought and freshness of insight. He is a writer of rare skill and dedication. In this his newest book I feel that there is evidence of a remarkable spiritual maturity. This volume is a veritable handbook of Christian truth which is greatly needed by church members, those not yet Christians and more mature Christians.

Jesus Christ said to Simon Peter, "I give you the keys to

the kingdom." He was referring to apostolic authority and to giving him the divinely directed insights concerning the laws and principles by which the kingdom of heaven actually functions on earth today. Dr. McBirnie has carefully researched these laws and the principles which need to be understood better. Heresies and apostasies cannot prevail when we are confronted with a scholarly study concerning the profound truths of the Word of God.

At the heart of all Dr. McBirnie has written is the necessity of full surrender to the Lordship of Jesus Christ at the very outset of conversion. Too often this is seen as a *future* consequence of accepting Christ into the life of the believer. The failure of thorough teaching of this truth to all new converts may be the explanation of why some falter and fail in the Christian life.

My advice to the reader is to read the whole book. The truths in it become plainer and more thrilling as the book progresses!

I am very pleased to commend this book to every Christian who desires a fuller life in Christ. It will be of great value to all preachers, teachers and Bible students.

Warren C. Hultgren, Ph.D.
Senior Minister, First Baptist Church
Tulsa, Oklahoma

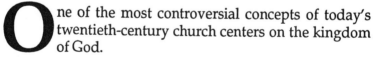

One of the most controversial concepts of today's twentieth-century church centers on the kingdom of God.

True to Dr. McBirnie's predictable style, he is unerringly faithful to the Scriptures, never deviating from biblical facts to fit the fads of the day. This volume will be timeless, as is the Bible.

The author of many books, perhaps this latest work will be a crowning classic. Scholarly in content with simplicity in style, the material is easy for the average layman to grasp.

Another interesting observation is Dr. McBirnie's unique ability to span religious denominations. The son of a prominent Presbyterian pastor and a graduate of one of America's most prestigious Baptist seminaries, we would consider him a conservative evangelical. The author founded the California Graduate School of Theology with graduates from almost every denomination around the world. Within this transdenominational background, the writer has taught several hundred lay people in a weekly Bible seminar in one of America's best known charismatic churches.

A gifted communicator, Dr. McBirnie hosts his long-running radio commentary, "Voice of Americanism," which is heard on a network of stations. Also, he is a featured regular guest of the Trinity Broadcasting Network.

For more than half a century, I have formed the habit of reading at least two books per week in addition to Bible studies. It is my belief that *Keys to the Kingdom* is destined to be a treasured text that should be in every personal library.

"A drop of ink can make millions think!"

Ralph Wilkerson
Pastor, Melodyland Christian Center
Anaheim, California

INTRODUCTION

Years ago I penned a brief study titled "What Became of the Twelve Apostles?" Recognizing the limitation of that project, based only on standard reference materials, I offered the hope that a scholar might sift through the mass of post-biblical information, legend, tradition and as yet unpublished material on the lives of the apostles and produce a credible, historically critical and definitive work on the probable biographies of the founders of the churches.

Decades passed, and no such study appeared, so I engaged upon the task. My resultant book, *The Search for the*

Twelve Apostles, has achieved wide distribution and critical acceptance as the standard work in that field.

In much the same way I have long known the need for a codifying of God's kingdom laws. Indeed, most preachers have dipped here and there into these universal principles. But to my knowledge no one has made a systematic compilation of them.

A few years before his death I suggested to E. Stanley Jones that he write such a book. So many of the laws of the kingdom appear in his devotional books that I felt he was the one who could do it successfully. As he writes in his introduction to *The Unshakable Kingdom and the Unchanging Person*, he accepted the challenge by taking a year to review the New Testament for an intensive analysis. By the end of that time he felt he needed to emphasize the person of Christ and the inseparable link with His kingdom. He produced insights with which I fully agree. However, I believe his age prevented him from breaking new ground.

So there remained a need for a compilation of the kingdom laws, a task I have taken on with this book. I do not pretend that this study is exhaustive. Without a doubt, others more able will add to or correct what I have pioneered. The important thing is to forge ahead lest we lose sight of the vast resources of the King, lest we fail to surrender to His principles as we live and work for our Lord Jesus Christ.

No parliament passes into legislation what we call physical laws. No collection of scientists decides what these laws shall be. They came into being with God's creation. They change not.

Likewise, we cannot invent spiritual laws, nor can we tinker with them.

Most physical laws are discovered by one person who thinks behind appearances to the principles which underlie them. Then he and others verify those principles. Only then can they begin to be accepted generally — because they can be universally verified — as "laws."

For example, the law of gravity describes how one mass attracts another, depending upon the relative size of each body. Gases expand at a rate determined by a law. Magnetic fields flow at a certain rate and behave according to negative and positive forces. Atomic particles behave according to certain laws of physics, functioning in some ways like tiny solar systems.

Physical law, then, is simply an accepted description of the way things are and work in nature. Obviously, from time to time descriptions of physical laws must be reappraised. Our knowledge grows, and some laws must be expanded; our description of the behavior of reality must be altered. It is not that the law is changing, but rather our understanding gradually comes into greater clarity.

Likewise, the laws of the kingdom of God do not change. This kingdom is as real as the physical universe, though beyond it. Only here and there does God's kingdom cross over and become visible to us. In the Bible, too, the curtain lifts for a moment, and we are granted a quick look at the all-powerful, joyous and very glorious universe of God.

Paul wrote, "The invisible things of him from the creation of the world are clearly seen, being understood by the things that are made, even his eternal power and Godhead" (Rom. 1:20). So which is reality? Our world, which is passing away and therefore changing constantly? Or the other world, which is ultimate reality?

Too many glimpses of that other world exist for us to deny its existence. Consequently, we must ask: Are there principles or laws of that other world which are at work and which can be grasped by us in this life? Of course there are. Otherwise the Bible is a book of useless hopes, and Jesus Christ is a mistaken and tragic figure.

C.S. Lewis figured there are only three explanations for Jesus Christ: He was a megalomaniac, claiming things not real. He was a cheat and a liar, teaching things not true. Or

He was God, showing Himself to mankind.

One cannot thoughtfully believe He was either insane or a deceiver because He is the standard for ideal behavior. Time has proven that what He did and said is ultimately righteous. Therefore He was God revealing Himself to man and redeeming man. *Jesus is that other world appearing in our world, urging us to live by the laws of the kingdom, which extend to both worlds.*

This book is intended to describe at least some of the laws of God's everlasting kingdom, which cannot be shaken. By "laws" I do not mean simply commandments such as are to be found in the decalogue God gave Moses. As we will see, Mosaic law was superseded: "The law was given by Moses, but grace and truth came by Jesus Christ" (John 1:17). Our hope lies not in merely returning to outward observances of commandments. Nor do I mean by "laws" mere rules of behavior for citizens of the kingdom of God, though this is somewhat closer. The Christian faith is more than adhering to suggested rules for obedience, happiness or success.

"Laws" in this study means *principles which we observe at work in the kingdom of God*. To perceive of the nature of reality is to know the laws of the kingdom.

How greatly we need to understand the true nature of our kingdom! How else can we be maximally effective for God except by knowing and obeying His laws?

Recent experiments with terminally ill patients have proved that positive mental attitudes have great power to postpone death, even to restore health. These studies show that some of the approaches of Christian Science and positive thinking really work. Unfortunately, the application of these principles has often been at the expense of a sound Christian theology.

This is a tragedy indeed because it need not be so. Christianity contains every one of the valid insights of positive mental attitudes. Where else did the "positive mentalists" get their ideas to begin with? But why pervert or throw out the great and everlasting truth of what C.S. Lewis called "classical Christianity" only to glean *some* of the fruits of Christianity's body of truth?

I impute no villainy to Christians who have selectively emphasized certain neglected principles of the kingdom of God. By the same token, those of us devoted to orthodox Christianity have not really preached the full gospel if we have neglected truths in the gospel that others have found more relevant to people's needs.

We *must* reoccupy forfeited ground while not forsaking the main citadel of our faith. We *must* resurvey the whole territory of the kingdom and not, as Paul reminded the elders at Ephesus, fail "to declare unto you *all* the counsel of God" (Acts 20:27, italics mine).

W.S. McBirnie, Ph.D.
President
The California Graduate School of Theology

PART 1

THE BATTLE OF WILLS

ONE

LETTING GOD USE YOU

The law of submission

Mash your car's brakes, and you've started a con-flict: The law of friction wars against the law of momentum. Whichever one prevails determines the outcome — whether the car will stop in time.

Of course, you don't consciously think: I'm going to release the law of friction to overcome the law of momentum before my car hurtles past that stop sign. But those laws are at work. And just as there are laws constantly operating in nature, so there are fixed laws in the kingdom of God.

God's kingdom will not arrive in its fullness until the

thousand-year reign of Christ. For now it exists wherever God is King. Wherever God does not reign, the kingdom cannot be found. So the kingdom ebbs and flows according to how much of our lives we bring under His lordship.

We are responsible to understand how the kingdom of God operates, what it is, what its rules and laws are. Consequently, the first and greatest kingdom law is the law of submission: *We must submit entirely to God's will to function in His kingdom.*

Tug-of-wills

We tend to classify people in categories based on our perceptions: the religious and the irreligious; the believer and the unbeliever; the righteous and the sinner. The Bible, however, focuses more on whether our religion consists of self-will or whether it is based on submission to God's will.

Anytime we do something that violates His kingdom's rules, that defies His lordship, we find ourselves in trouble because the kingdom operates only through our being submissive to His will. Rebelling against His will places us outside the kingdom.

Because of the strong pull of self-will, all men give their highest allegiance to something, if not God. Whatever they obey, work for, belong to and serve is their god. It can be money, people or pleasure; it can be a system of government or philosophy. But every man serves and, in effect, worships something apart from himself. "For none of us liveth to himself, and no man dieth to himself" (Rom. 14:7).

Therefore the existence of atheists — those completely rejecting all deities — does not line up with Scripture. Or, alternately, *mere religion is not the hallmark of the righteous man.* The issue is between right religion and wrong religion. To the world, anybody who goes to a church and makes a profession of faith is automatically religious. But religion or the lack thereof has little to do with obeying God's will.

The bankruptcy of classifying people as religious or irreligious is evident when you realize that those perceived as the most religious people in the first century were the Pharisees, the Sadducees, the priests and the Levites. No Roman was ever as pious as the average Jew. No Roman priest was as pious as a Jewish priest. Yet it was those religious Jews who crucified the Son of God and persecuted the early church.

There is an even more subtle difference in the case of Judaism: The religion itself was not surrendered to the will of God. Otherwise the Jews would have welcomed His Son with open arms. By seizing the externals of religion, they were able to maintain a façade that fooled others and even themselves, but which masked what Hebrews 3:12 calls "an evil heart of unbelief." We can appear to be serving God but actually be hating Him. We can perform rituals in His honor, but dishonor Him through inward rebellion. This was the sin of the Jews of Jesus' day. It remains our sin today.

Here is the heart of the matter: Are we trying to use God, or are we trying to let God use us? Newspaper church pages advertise sermon topics that appear to be very religious. But in actuality the messages often exalt the preachers and ignore God, or they tickle people's fancies with the notion that they can use God to get what they want if only they discover the formula. On the contrary, *letting God use us* is the key to the law of submission.

Prayer, Pride and Power

This law can be better understood through three words beginning with "p": prayer, pride and power.

In the heart of the Lord's prayer we find how prayer relates to this law:

After this manner therefore pray ye: Our Father which art in heaven, hallowed be thy name. Thy

Begins and ends with submission to God.

kingdom come. Thy will be done in earth, as it is in heaven. Give us this day our daily bread. And forgive us our debts, as we forgive our debtors. And lead us not into temptation, but deliver us from evil: For thine is the kingdom, and the power, and the glory, for ever. Amen" (Matt. 6:9-13).

The first section deals entirely with submission to the will of God. "Hallowed be thy name." "Thy kingdom come." "Thy will be done in earth, as it is in heaven." Only then does the prayer turn to petitions, asking for daily bread and so forth. But then it reaffirms kingdom themes, ascribing to God the fullness of His kingdom, power and glory. *The prayer begins with submission to God and then returns to submission to God.*

We miss the spirit of this prayer unless we understand the enthusiasm implied in the original manuscript. It is not: "Lord, I suppose Your will has to be done. It is pretty painful, but I guess, Lord, Your will should be done here just as it is in heaven." Instead it is: "Lord, Thy will be done!" The prayer illustrates the necessity of embracing the will of God. The disciples had asked, "Lord, teach us to pray." So He emphasized doing the Father's will.

A second element illustrating the law of complete submission to God's will is pride. It's been said there is hardly anything God won't let you do if you will not take the credit. Isaiah 42:8 puts it this way: "I am the Lord: that is my name: and my glory will I not give to another." The moment we reach out to grab credit that belongs to the Lord, we are in deadly danger, just as if we had put forth our hand to touch the ark of the covenant.

Jesus said to pray: *Thine* is the kingdom; *Thine* is the power; *Thine* is the glory. But this is often how we translate it: *Thine* is the kingdom; *Thine* is the power; *mine* is the glory.

There is an inward spirit that constantly seeks to push God off His throne and to seat self on the throne of life. But pride is dethroned when we pray, "*Thine* is the glory."

The third illustration involves God's power, which can do what we cannot do. Jesus declared, "For thine is the kingdom and the power." The word "power" is not only ability and strength, but authority. God's authority shall reign instead of ours.

Much of our lives is spent searching for and seizing power. Why? So we won't have to pray "Thine is the power." That is why so many people in religion seek power. They love the power of popularity; they seek ecclesiastical power; they strive for high office, fame and money — all because they want power. In doing so they violate the law of absolute submission to the will of God, the seat of all power. "Not by might, nor by power, but by my spirit, saith the Lord of hosts" (Zech. 4:6).

Whose Interests First?

We must ask ourselves: Do I — through religion or prayer, in the exercise of power or indulging in pride — seek to use God to my ends? Or do I let God use me to His ends? The Bible calls us the *servants* of God, not the *masters* of God. My role is not to tell God what to do. My role is to do what God tells me to do.

Paul began some of his epistles with this phrase: "Paul, a servant of Jesus Christ." *Slave* would be a more accurate rendering than "servant." The Greek word connotes something stark, simple, almost brutal. Paul, a man without will of his own; Paul, a man who belongs to Jesus, not himself; Paul, a man who works for the Master and not for his own welfare; Paul, a man who understood the necessity of submission to the will of God.

What about our prayer life? Do we eagerly seek the will of God? Or are we trying to get God to be a partner to something we have already decided?

There is nothing wrong with buying and selling or getting

gain. But in our worry to control our own success, sometimes a little heavenly insurance seems attractive. "Lord, I'm already involved in this; please come along and help me." James warned us about this attitude. "Go to now, ye that say, To day or to morrow we will go into such a city...and buy and sell, and get gain" (James 4:13). He corrected us, "Ye ought to say, If the Lord will, we shall live, and do this, or that" (v. 15).

It is even possible for me to try to use God when I am preaching His Word. Suppose I pray, "Lord, please help me to preach this sermon well." That is dead wrong. I am trying to use God. What I should pray is, "Lord, Your people are gathering with hungry hearts, and they hope they will hear from You today. Now, Lord, I have no wisdom to share with them, but You have great wisdom and great resources; You love them. For Your own glory, for Your own purposes, *use me* as Your servant through whom the Word of God may be clearly proclaimed!"

That attitude does not try to use God to help me but puts me at His disposal. This is a subtle distinction in some cases, but drastically different from the average approach to prayer. Once this truth is mastered, it reaches to the very roots of our being and provides us a yardstick by which we can gauge the rightness or wrongness of our behavior, our decisions and our thoughts. It guides us through the decisions of life because we are getting God's direction instead of God's occasional blessing on our best guesses. It rids us forever of simplistic, easy answers that are of Satan and the world, answers that fail to tell us the truth about ourselves.

Prayer in the spirit of the Lord's prayer — that *Thy* will be done — is a critical part of fulfilling this primary law of submission. Unless we are continually praying for God's will, we will never live it fully. And as the next chapter will show, God's will is not some unsolvable mystery but something He desires to reveal to us.

22

TWO

LOOKING FOR YOUR BROOK CHERITH

The law of finding the will of God

As I traveled through Europe, the swarming multitudes made me realize the planet groans with the weight of five billion human beings. I could not help but ask myself about the relationship of the gospel to all these people, to these diverse civilizations built around various Christian denominations and a plethora of religions and contemporary ideas.

What is it that differentiates the Christian message from all others? I wondered. What is the one essential that men and women must understand to be saved?

And I opened my Bible to the words of Jesus. They stood out as if written in letters of fire: "Not every one that saith unto me, Lord, Lord, shall enter into the kingdom of heaven; but he that doeth the will of my Father which is in heaven" (Matt. 7:21).

There, in the conclusion of the Sermon on the Mount, is the litmus test for membership in God's kingdom in words simple enough for a child to understand. Not everyone who professes religion, not everyone who can phrase eloquent prayers in the pulpit, not everyone who says, "I am religious," not every professor of theology shall enter God's kingdom. As the old Negro spiritual says, "Everybody talking about heaven ain't going there."

This principle is evidenced from the Bible's opening pages. Adam's son Abel brought a more acceptable sacrifice to the Lord than did his brother, Cain. Cain's so-called sacrifice was probably nice. Perhaps he brought the best pumpkins that grew in his field. But God had not asked for pumpkins; He wanted a sacrifice that would remind man that sin is very real, corrosive and damaging; that sin had brought about a rupture in the relationship between God and man.

Abel, meanwhile, brought a lamb. By its death, by its symbolic shedding of blood, the lamb sacrifice matched the seriousness of sin.

Cain substituted his own interpretation for the realities of God's kingdom. That's why the Bible speaks about substituting our own ideas for God's ideas as "the way of Cain."

And that's why Jesus said the one who will enter the kingdom of heaven is "he that *doeth the will of my Father*." Of course, that condition may raise few objections until we face the flip side of the coin: We must first forsake our will to do His will. And here is where the distinction is so clear between Christianity and many other religions. They say, "Bend God to do *your* will," or "God is dead," or "Old ideas of God have disappeared. The important thing is to be whole and happy."

More important than happiness — though surprisingly, it is the only source of lasting joy, of true fulfillment — is to do the will of God. Jesus defined His coming in these terms: "My meat is to do the will of him that sent me" (John 4:34).

Since we are called to be molded after Christ, this is our purpose also. It is summed up in the law of finding the will of God: *God intends for each of His children to discover His will and do it.*

Elijah and the Will of God

You may be about to buy a house or considering enrolling in a school. Perhaps you are mulling over a career change.

Sincere Christians want to make these decisions based on God's will; yet they often are puzzled as to how to find it. Let's examine the story of Elijah, which provides answers to the universal challenge of discovering God's will. You may not have the prophetic ministry Elijah had, but you should expect no less revelation from God concerning His will for your life.

Elijah told wicked King Ahab of God's impending judgment: "As the Lord God of Israel liveth, before whom I stand, there shall not be dew nor rain these years, but according to my word" (1 Kin. 17:1).

Some time passed, "And the word of the Lord came unto him, saying, Get thee hence, and turn thee eastward, and hide thyself by the brook Cherith, that is before Jordan. And it shall be, that thou shalt drink of the brook; and I have commanded the ravens to feed thee there" (1 Kin. 17:2-4).

The ravens brought Elijah bread and flesh in the morning and in the evening, and he drank of the water of the brook. But after a while the brook dried up because of the drought.

> And the word of the Lord came unto him, saying, Arise, get thee to Zarephath, which belongeth to

Zidon, and dwell there: behold, I have commanded a widow woman there to sustain thee. So he arose and went to Zarephath (1 Kin. 17:8-10).

This was in the opposite direction, and Elijah knew it was a pagan land. Nevertheless, he obeyed God. When he came to the gate of Zarephath, the widow was there gathering sticks. He said:

Fetch me, I pray thee, a little water in a vessel, that I may drink. And as she was going to fetch it, he called to her, and said, Bring me, I pray thee, a morsel of bread in thine hand. And she said, As the Lord thy God liveth, I have not a cake, but an handful of meal in a barrel, and a little oil in a cruse: and, behold, I am gathering two sticks, that I may go in and dress it for me and my son, that we may eat it, and die. And Elijah said unto her, Fear not; go and do as thou hast said: but make me thereof a little cake first, and bring it unto me, and after make for thee and for thy son. For thus saith the Lord God of Israel, the barrel of meal shall not waste, neither shall the cruse of oil fail, until the day that the Lord sendeth rain upon the earth. And she went and did according to the saying of Elijah: and she, and he, and her house, did eat many days. And the barrel of meal wasted not, neither did the cruse of oil fail, according to the word of the Lord, which he spake by Elijah" (1 Kin. 17:10-16).

Step-by-Step

The will of God was to preserve Elijah through the drought, but first God revealed only phase one — that the drought was coming. This is a basic principle of finding

God's will: *God usually reveals His will one step at a time.*

Later He revealed that Elijah was to go down to the brook and be fed by the ravens, but nothing further was shown. Still later God revealed that He had provided the most unlikely means of support — a widow and ravens to feed Elijah.

Here is perhaps the greatest prophet who ever lived, but he did not see very far into the future. The next step — that is about all that God will reveal to you or to me, except under unusual circumstances. We would like to see the full plan outlined, with names, dates and places, as well as insurance contracts to hedge our risks. God just says no. He doesn't work that way.

But it's not that He's cruel; rather God knows that if He showed us the full plan, we would take shortcuts or frustrate His plan or try to change it. So just as a fisherman reels in his line — one turn at a time — God unfolds His plans for us one day at a time.

The Role of Prayer

Were you to read only the account of Elijah going before the king, you might be led to think Elijah was presumptuous, even arrogant, to stride into the king's court, saying, "When I say the rain is going to stop, it is going to stop. When I say it is going to begin, it is going to begin."

However, James 5:17-18 puts Elijah's bold statements in perspective: "Elias was a man subject to like passions as we are, and he prayed earnestly that it might not rain: and it rained not on the earth by the space of three years and six months. And he prayed again, and the heaven gave rain, and the earth brought forth her fruit."

Elijah's secret was that he was a man of prayer. If you want sincerely to find and do the will of God, you too must go through the avenue of prayer. Not only prayer that God will guide you, but prayer that is sincerely desirous of the will of God. Not prayer that your will may be done — with hope that God will bend His will to yours — but prayer that seeks His will no matter what the consequences may be.

We are afraid that if we honestly say, "O God, Thy will be done in me as it is in heaven," God will ask us to make a sacrifice we cannot bear to make or to carry out an errand we dare not run. The subconscious implication is that God is cruel. This is Satan's lie, for the Bible equates God with love. It is only when you believe with all your heart that God is love that you are emboldened to pray, "O Lord, Thy will be done."

As Elijah sought to do God's will, he was forced — as we should be — to keep himself in the center of the will of God. When God told Elijah to go down to the brook Cherith, he may have objected, but God said he had commanded ravens to feed him twice a day *there* — not at Jericho, not at Jerusalem, not in Samaria, not even in Zidon, but at the brook Cherith. Had Elijah gone somewhere other than the center of God's will, the ravens would have been on time but Elijah would have gone hungry.

R.A. Torrey, the first superintendent of Moody Bible Institute, said in his book *How to Pray* (Moody Press) that the only way we can get our prayers answered is for us to be on praying ground. This means to be in the place where God's blessing is promised.

After the brook dried up, God said He wanted Elijah to go to a heathen land, as He had commanded a widow to sustain him there. When Elijah went to the place where God indicated, the Lord revealed His will and provided Elijah with sustenance that saved him through the drought.

Elijah found the will of God and did it. He exercised active faith, not passive faith. I believe he went joyously to the brook, joyously to the widow's house. Probably he never would have vacationed in either place had it been up to him. But he never considered his plans as being up to him. It was God's will he was seeking and doing.

In the same way, we are to pursue God's will actively: "O God, what is Your will? I embrace it. I love it. Lord, such is my confidence in You and in Your love. If this is what You desire for me, it is my fondest wish."

To Do the Will of God

How then do you *know* and *do* the will of God?

First, you seek it. It will not be found by wondering. Jesus was as clear as He could be: "Seek, and ye shall find" (Matt. 7:7b). Matt. 6:33

The best place to search is in the Bible. The Scriptures exist for one reason paramount to all others: to show us the will of God. People of great faith and great prayer, people whom God has chosen to give power to work miracles, are always familiar with God's Word. They stay close to the Bible. They plot their course by it. They pray according to its promises.

If we pray for *anything, according to His will*, God hears us, Put on and we can know we have the petitions desired (1 John 5:14-15). To know the will of God and to pursue it, then, is the secret of successful prayer. Having found God's will, praying is easy, quick and direct. If your prayers have not been answered, the reason may lie here. God cannot work contrary to His will.

How have men had the power to die for Jesus Christ? How have they endured torment and suffering? How have so many laid aside every human ambition and served God alone in the heat of the fiery furnace? How have men made sacrifices so astounding in comparison to those most of us make that we are made ashamed to read of them?

It is just one thing! They chose to do the will of God above their own will. This was the secret of Christ's life. This is the secret of the life of every successful Christian. The degree to which we are willing to harmonize our lives, wills and thoughts with the will of God is the degree to which we are successful Christians.

29

Zeroing in on God's Will

Satan strikes blows against God's kingdom as long as he can keep you from God's will. His strategies are clever, often subtle. Let me suggest a four-point prayer to help you focus on the perfect will of God for every area of your life:

Lord, save me from rebellion, for rebellion is rejection of the will of God and the substitution of my own stubborn will.

Lord, save me from heresy, which is the substitution of a false, religious interpretation of the will of God for His real will. It matters not what the heresy is. It always amounts to a counterfeit will of God.

Lord, save me from rationalization, which is my attempt to explain away the will of God. For example, the will of God is that His people tithe, but some rationalize that they don't have to by postulating that tithing was meant only for the Jews.

Lord, deliver me from willing ignorance of Your will. When I was a boy, my mother would leave instructions for what I was to do after school on a slip of paper under the sugar bowl. I had the clever idea that if I didn't run across the note, being ignorant of what it told me to do, I would not be held responsible. I wasted more time trying to devise a way to go through the house and get what I needed without having to pass through the kitchen.

As silly as that sounds, even we adults enjoy practicing the same self-deception. We reason that if we can just remain ignorant of certain things God would have us do, we can escape the responsibility of following God's will. Willing ignorance! We can achieve it only through our willful evasiveness.

After praying these four points with all sincerity, you can expect God to be faithful to help you to know His will, to love His will and to do His will. You can confess, as Jesus did, "My meat is to do the will of him that sent me, and to finish his work" (John 4:34).

THREE

MAN'S FLIGHT PATTERN

The law of man's natural tendency

The greatest sin is not murder, though it is heinous. The greatest sin is not that of betrayal to one's country, though that's a monstrous crime, so designated by both Old and New Testaments.

These sins are abominable to God. But the greatest sin is rebellion against God, refusal to love and seek Him.

This is not something man has to work up to. He naturally wants to escape from God and hide. This is the law of man's natural tendency: *Man's nature is to run away from God, not toward Him*. Man does have a religious side, but it does not

31

overrule this basic law. Isaiah put it well: "All we like sheep have gone astray; we have turned every one to his own way" (Is. 53:6).

Leave Us Alone

Our Creator made us to function in fellowship with Him, and He alone possesses the right and ability to guide us into the best plan for our lives. But if we are unwilling to do what He wants us to do, we disrupt His plan. We will not fulfill our destiny.

We set up rebellion against Him, which is sin. Sin is not only social misbehavior. We can keep the laws of the land perfectly and yet sin grievously by violating the laws and will of God.

It is sometimes preached that all people are seeking God. That's ridiculous. While everyone has a need for God, and therefore what you might call a religious bent, they also wish that God had nothing in mind for them. They simply want to go their own way, just as Isaiah said.

When Jesus came to the Golan Heights, He found two wild men in a cemetery. The hideous demons inside one of the men cried out, "What have we to do with thee, Jesus, thou Son of God?" (Matt. 8:29). In the presence of God these devils were panic-stricken, basically saying to Jesus, "Leave us alone; our time has not yet come."

Leave us alone. That too is exactly the primary request unregenerate man makes of God.

This nature is present even in the youngest of children. Don't be fooled into thinking it isn't present just because your child enjoys attending church. Very young children often like church because they have some fun with the Bible stories, the singing, the get-togethers, the crafts and games. But when they reach the teen years and their self-awareness increases, many move away from the church. Why? Because of the tendency to flee from God. The only ones who stay are those who truly have come to know Christ as Savior and Lord.

This universal tendency to run from God can be overcome by strong biblical teaching and the power of the Holy Spirit. Young people need a strong foundation in their prayer lives. They must be trained to fellowship with God so they can learn to revere Him, to know what He desires for them.

A Faithful Shepherd

Fortunately, there is a flip side to this pattern of flight: *While man is not seeking God, God is seeking man.*

C.S. Lewis, the great British author and theologian, was once an atheist. He couldn't stand the thought of being a Christian. One day he came face-to-face with his Creator:

> You must picture me alone in that room in Oxford University night after night feeling whenever my mind lifted even for a second from my work, the steady, unrelenting approach of Him whom I so earnestly desired not to meet. That which I greatly feared had at last come upon me.

Lewis accepted Christ that night in 1929. In retrospect, recalling his own attitude about giving in to the God who had pursued him so relentlessly, he arrived at a deeper understanding of God's nature:

> I did not then see what is now the most shining and obvious thing, the divine humility which will accept a convert even on such terms. The prodigal son at least walked home on his own feet, but who can duly adore that love which will open the high gates to a prodigal who is brought in kicking, struggling, resentful, darting his eyes in every direction for a chance of escape. The words *compel*

them to come in have been so abused by wicked men that we shudder at them, but more properly understood they plumb the depth of the divine mercy. The hardness of God is kinder than the softness of men, and his compulsion is our liberation.

Our loving God hounded this man, an atheist who didn't want anything to do with God. Lewis couldn't escape from the magnetic pull of God's love.

The truth that God bothers to seek His turncoat creatures in love makes Christianity different from false religions centered on man's seeking to placate God. In those religions man in effect seeks to bribe God, to influence Him.

But Christianity does not allow that. It teaches that though man flees from God, God is seeking man. Only in Christianity is this truth revealed: that God was in Christ reconciling the world unto Himself. As Jesus said in Luke 19:10: "The Son of man is come to seek and to save that which was lost."

How can anybody ever find God if he is running away from Him? In truth, God finds man. God sets up certain conditions in the world — trouble is one of them — as part of this process. He also uses the awareness of His presence, the fact that He is a God of moral justice ruling over a moral universe and that we cannot go against the laws of God without eventually breaking ourselves. God is standing above life and behind life and under life and beyond life, and therefore sooner or later we are going to confront Him. These things make us keenly aware that God is searching for us, and thus we become aware of our need to reckon with Him.

Before Adam and Eve sinned, God would come down in the cool of the evening and walk with them and talk with them. They were glad to see Him. But after they sinned, they hid themselves. And what was the question God asked that fateful evening when He came down to be with His creatures? He cried out, "Adam, where art thou?" Up to this point man had come seeking for God. But the very moment that man sinned, he hid from God — and he has been doing that ever since.

At the same time, however, God continued to seek Adam. Even today God comes after man, asking, "Where art thou?"

The Adversary Fallacy

In some cases where communists have infiltrated African countries, they bribe village witch doctors to tell the natives that they should cooperate only with the communist revolutionaries. Consequently, the native government has the ridiculous task of paying tremendous sums of money to the witch doctors to prevent them from influencing the people the wrong way.

What sort of religion does this boil down to? It's not love of God but rather a tug-of-war with God, trying to persuade Him not to curse them. While bribing witch doctors may seem a bit removed from our experience, the root issue is no different from man's attitude throughout the world. Most religion amounts to little more than ceremonially telling God, "Get off my back."

That is religion. But it is not Christianity. It is only a reflection of the law of man's natural tendency, which predicts man will flee from God. This distorted view of God as the adversary, the One who is out to get them, is evident in our insurance claims, which call fires, earthquakes and other natural disasters "acts of God."

But Christians, too, often are guilty of resisting God. How many times do we pray, "Lord, stop Your punishment," when God is actually seeking to help us? God is more anxious to deliver us, to hear our prayers, than we are to have them answered or to be helped.

What kind of people is God looking for? Those who spend

a lifetime in self-torture or self-discipline to be old and wise enough finally to understand God? No. We are to receive God as little children. Jesus said, "Suffer the little children to come unto me...for of such is the kingdom of God" (Mark 10:14). He says, "I stand at the door, and knock: if any man hear my voice, and open the door, I will come in to him" (Rev. 3:20).

What a contrast with religions that demand that their adherents hire the priests, participate in the ceremonies, approach the temple — and maybe the gods will hear you. Our God's desire is to capture as many fleeing men as He can so He may bring many of His children to glory.

Spinning Out of Control

This law is also at work in people who have come under conviction for their sins and have begun to turn toward God. Working against them is a force pulling them away from God. Basically this is the law of man's natural tendency, but in this case it could be called the centrifugal law of human nature.

Centrifugal force is the tendency of anything that is revolving to fly outward from the center, just as occupants in a car will feel themselves pulled in one direction if the car turns a corner too quickly. Spiritually, God is the center of the universe and should be the focus of our lives. But life's cares and concerns, plus our selfish desires, propel us away from Him as we revolve through the years.

This centrifugal law operates in the life of a Christian, no matter how long one has walked with God. Even Paul experienced great difficulty in fully surrendering to God: "For I delight in the law of God after the inward man: But I see another law in my members, warring against the law of my mind, and bringing me into captivity to the law of sin which is in my members" (Rom. 7:22-23).

Paul recognized two laws at work. One was that God had

become his great delight, and Paul desired to serve Him and worship Him in every way. But even in the midst of his Christian walk Paul discerned a sinister law: that when he would like to do good, evil was ever-present with him. Consequently, the good he wanted to do he did not; and the evil he wished not to do, that he did.

We all know what Paul is talking about. It's why we turn over in our warm beds on Sunday morning and murmur, "I need to sleep in today." Yet we know the commandment of Hebrews 10:25 is not to forsake the assembling of the church.

We are tempted to speak ill of others, though Jesus commanded, "Judge not, that ye be not judged" (Matt. 7:1). Our human tendency to rebel against God pulls us away from what He demands.

This law of ever-present evil applies to our pocketbooks. The bills are pretty heavy this month, we may say to ourselves. I don't believe I can afford to make my offering to God. Our lives may be spinning at one thousand revolutions per minute, with the centrifugal force of financial demands all but ripping us apart, but things are quite still at the center, where God reigns. And His Word says to bring the tithes into the storehouse. The tithe is holy unto the Lord. It isn't ours to start with.

Satan takes what you would do naturally then pulls you relentlessly toward it. The devil wants you forever alienated from God. How quick he is to bring all sorts of inducements, rationalizations and explanations to do what we want to do instead of what God wants us to do.

How then do we overcome Satan working through our own natural tendency to flee from God? Through prayer. That's why the Bible says to pray every day, to be in constant contact with God.

What would we think of a soldier who fought in a war day after day but never attempted to contact headquarters? How would he know where to fight? He would soon be isolated and killed. He needs to stay in touch with headquarters so he can get his orders for the day. We do that through prayer, reading and meditating on the Scriptures and taking responsibility for our place, however big or small it may be, in the kingdom of God.

FOUR

ADAM'S LEGACY

The law of the origin of sin

I magine doing a survey with this one question: "Our preacher was talking about sin this morning," you say. "What do *you* think sin is?"

You would be surprised at the ignorant replies you would get. Why? Because most people have no firm concept of sin.

Mention sinners and many people think of the criminal class or those who are engaged in extreme forms of social misbehavior. Yet sin has very little to do with just one type of behavior. Sin starts within and then progresses outward. Sin is an attitude that begins in the heart. Jesus said that which defiles a man is not that which comes from without and goes within, such as what he eats or drinks. Rather it is that which begins in the heart and proceeds outward, resulting in sinful actions (Matt. 15:17-20).

That process reveals the law of the origin of sin: *Sin results from the selfish desires in our hearts that we inherit from Adam.*

Sin, in the simplest definition, is the violation of the revealed will of God. "Revealed will" because we cannot follow God's will unless it becomes clear to us through the Bible or prayer. A person can keep the law of the land and yet be a horrible sinner, because civil law is not the same thing as God's law. Whatever God reveals for mankind in general, or as His will for our life in particular, He expects us to do. James states clearly what it means to dodge what God has revealed: "Therefore to him that knoweth to do good, and doeth it not, to him it is sin" (James 4:17).

For example, it is God's will that we revere the Lord's day. The Old Testament Sabbath, observed on Saturday, was a day of rest. The Lord's day, established since the days of the early church as Sunday, is one of intense devotion and works for the kingdom of God. It is the Christian's responsibility to give God first place on the Lord's day or else risk sinning.

Sin's Origins

Knowing where sin came from won't cure it, just as the knowledge of what causes cancer will not by itself cure the cancer. But if we can understand sin's historical and personal origins, as well as the sin process, it will better enable us to receive help from the Great Physician, who can cure what we cannot.

Paul wrote, "By the law is the knowledge of sin" (Rom. 3:20). On the other hand, there is no knowledge of sin where there is no law. He was referring to the law of God — revealed in the Old Testament and the New Testament —

and also the universal law of God written on every heart. So no one is without sin because no one is born without at least some fundamental knowledge of the law of God.

For example, C.S. Lewis said every race of people has considered it wrong to steal. Some tribes in the primitive areas of the world think it's all right to steal from enemies, but even they don't think it's right to steal from their friends. At this basic level there exists universal law, etched into hearts, that stealing is wrong. And it is by the law, in whatever form, that sin is known.

In Luke 10:18 Jesus said He saw Satan fall as lightning to the earth. So the first sin of which we have any record occurred in heaven. Isaiah 14:12-14 elaborates:

> How art thou fallen from heaven, O Lucifer, son of the morning! how art thou cut down to the ground, which didst weaken the nations! For thou hast said in thine heart, I will ascend into heaven, I will exalt my throne above the stars of God: I will sit also upon the mount of the congregation, in the sides of the north: I will ascend above the heights of the clouds; I will be like the most High.

Lucifer was the brightest, the strongest, the wisest of the angels. He was the sum of God's creation. One day when his heart was lifted up in pride, he announced, "I will be like the most High." Five times in this passage Lucifer affirmed, "I will." The first sin in the universe was willfulness, and it is still the major sin. A third of the angels of God were deceived by this angel and were cast out of heaven with him (Rev. 12:4).

Man's first sin was committed in the Garden of Eden when Adam and Eve violated the revealed will of God. Because we share Adam and Eve's humanity, we share their willfulness. Romans 5:12 explains: "Wherefore, as by one man sin entered into the world, and death by sin; and so death passed upon all men, for that all have sinned."

Drawn to Sin

This Adamic nature predisposes us to sin. To this truth many parents can readily say amen.

Many godly parents raise their children to be Christians. They teach them to pray before they can read. They take them to Sunday school and church, but in the teen years the children reject the church and God. The bewildered parents ask, "What did we do wrong? Where did we go astray?"

Part of the answer lies in the inherited nature of Adam, which is willful, proud and naturally at enmity with God. No Christian education, no training in a Christian home, can remove the Adamic nature. We can train a tiger as much as we want, but he remains a tiger. We can train a human being as much as we like, even in a Christian way — which we should do — but that training won't change his nature. Therefore it is no surprise when the child asserts his will and chooses to sin.

So what can Christian parents do? We are not only to train our children in Christianity, but we are to explain to them the nature of sin and its remedy, so that they can choose for themselves to belong to Christ. They will choose to sin until they surrender their lives to Christ.

The second sense in which we have an origin of sin is that Satan or his emissaries — demons, as the Bible calls them — provoke and tempt us to sin.

Third, fleshly impulses provoke us to sin. The Bible calls these impulses the lusts of the flesh. James 1:14-15 presents the clearest statement of this aspect: "But every man is tempted, when he is drawn away of his own lust, and enticed. Then when lust hath conceived, it bringeth forth sin: and sin, when it is finished, bringeth forth death."

Sin starts as lust, a desire for something we should not have. It may be illicit sex, drinking, excessive eating, possessions, pride, property, fame or money.

What makes the difference between a legitimate desire for money and a sinful desire? When we want money for the glory of God and to do the normal things of life that He wants us to enjoy, the desire for money is consonant with the Bible. Deuteronomy 8:18 says the Lord gives us the power to gain wealth. The Bible commends thrift, investment and reward.

But if we desire money for our own aggrandizement or pride, we have a lust for money. James warns that after lust has conceived, it births sin, and sin ends in death.

Sin's Remedy

Since all of us have a sin nature, we need help to get off this fast track toward death. There are three stages in the cure for sin.

The first is *repentance*. Repentance means more than feeling sorry for our sins. True repentance is to change our minds about the attraction of sin and the consideration of sinning. Repentance is sorrow coupled with a changing of the mind.

Second, *we must admit our wrongdoing* — with no excuses. If we have done wrong against man, we may need to go to our brother and confess. But we need also to go to God and confess.

The third step to rid ourselves of sin is *to exercise faith in God's promise of forgiveness* by the blood of Jesus Christ. It is essential, however, that we truly believe God's forgiveness and, knowing that, that we forgive ourselves. Some of the most unhappy people are those who can't forgive themselves because they don't really believe God has forgiven them.

Our families, friends and enemies may not forgive and forget. But God offers this incredible promise that He will not only forgive but also forget.

It is the Lord's will for us to be forgiving, and sometimes this is much harder than accepting God's forgiveness. Some Christians live a kind of double life. They are very interested in winning souls to Christ, but they themselves are filled with "the gall of bitterness" (Acts 8:23) because of relationships with others.

How can we win somebody to Christ when Christ in us hasn't been manifested? We are in essence trying to sell something that we ourselves don't have. If we are actively receiving and giving forgiveness, we can present ourselves as vessels of righteousness, fit for use by the Lord.

Then we can overcome the law of the origin of sin through a higher power. Paul described it this way: "For the law of the Spirit of life in Christ Jesus hath made me free from the law of sin and death" (Rom. 8:2). The law of sin and death is absolute, affecting every person who enters the world. But thanks be to God, we do not have to remain under its domain forever.

As the next chapter will show, we inherit rights in a new family when we are delivered from the law of sin and death. Though that family may be large, many people would be surprised to learn how exclusive it is.

FIVE

FATHERLESS CHILDREN

The law of the sons of man and the sons of God

A prominent Southern governor admitted he had changed his attitude toward blacks. He said he had no ill will toward any man because we are all "children of God."

Rubbish! Of course, there is no difference in God's eyes between white men and black men. But this governor's theology is that of the man on the street, not of the Bible.

Nowhere does the gospel tell all men that they are children of God. On the contrary, the Scriptures affirm just the opposite.

45

The feel-good philosophy expounded by the governor so subtly pervades our society that it is worth bringing into the open. The law of the sons of man and the sons of God clears up this lie of universal sonship: *Man is alienated from God the Father until he is grafted into sonship through the inborn life of God's Son, Jesus Christ.*

Objects of Wrath

Jesus was born of the virgin Mary that He might bring many sons to glory (Heb. 2:10). He came that He might bring us out of mere humanity into sonship with God. Jesus became the Son of man in Bethlehem that we might become the sons of God upon conversion. "Glory" in Hebrews 2:10 is a synonym for the eternal joy the redeemed people will experience with God.

This was no small favor. Paul explained, "Among whom also we all had our conversation in times past in the lusts of our flesh, fulfilling the desires of the flesh and of the mind; and were by nature the children of wrath, even as others" (Eph. 2:3). Before conversion, the Ephesians by their very nature were objects of the wrath of God. Nevertheless, "even when we were dead in sins, [God] hath quickened us together with Christ, (by grace ye are saved)" (Eph. 2:5).

All Christians were once children of wrath. We were dead in trespasses and sins. We were cut off from the source of true life. We had physical life, but we didn't have spiritual life.

Once we are God's children, "we are his workmanship, created in Christ Jesus unto good works, which God hath before ordained that we should walk in them" (Eph. 2:10). We don't perform good works to be saved, but after we receive Christ they become the products of His work in us. God transforms us from children of wrath into the children of God, the objects of His workmanship.

Useless Reformation

In contrast to this biblical description of man before and after conversion is the pernicious doctrine that all men, simply by being born into the human family, are children of God.

Such a doctrine comes from Satan and misguided people. It assumes that the only change needed, or even possible for anyone, is reformation. If we are already children of God, then we are already as close to God as we can get. All one needs, perhaps, is to reform.

Jesus taught the folly of that idea. Luke 11 tells the story of a man who reformed and had an unclean spirit cast out but did not make a decision to follow God. The unclean spirit left but returned a few days later to a clean house (or soul). So the demon got seven other demons worse than he and moved back in. The man's end was worse than it had been before.

John 3:3 explains the true gospel, the only means to a permanent reformation: "Jesus answered and said unto him, Verily, verily, I say unto thee, Except a man be born again, he cannot see the kingdom of God." If we are already children of God by human birth, why would we need to be born again? "That which is born of the flesh is flesh; and that which is born of the Spirit is spirit" (John 3:6).

This doctrine of universal sonship comes in part from the state churches of Europe, where the king or queen is the head of the church. Or in other cases the state recognizes one particular religion or denomination as the official religion.

All state churches practice infant baptism because citizenship and being a Christian are held to be inseparable. Consequently, church officials sprinkle some water on babies' heads to christen them. The word "christen" means "to make a Christian."

When I was a week or two old, my parents took me to the church where my father was pastor, and he sprinkled some water on my head. I didn't know what sin, salvation, heaven or hell were, but I was supposedly a Christian.

That's pure folly. We need to be old enough to decide whether we want to follow Christ. *We must reach the age of accountability, know what sin is and who Jesus is, and exercise our wills to put our trust in Him.* One cannot passively enter the kingdom of God by the well-intentioned actions of another.

Creator to All, Father to Some

Perhaps the greatest reason for the wide belief in the doctrine of universal sonship is a failure to distinguish between God as Father and God as Creator. God created the trees, but He's not the Father of the trees. In the same way, He created man, but He's not the Father of all men. "They which are the children of the flesh, these are not the children of God" (Rom. 9:8).

We need to be born again because flesh and blood cannot inherit the kingdom of God. However, all men can *become* children of God and thereby enter into the inheritance. There is no barrier of race, culture or education.

The universal Fatherhood of God destroys the validity of evangelism and missionary work. If people are already children of God, all our evangelistic efforts can do is improve their outer man. But if they are not children of God, evangelism has a purpose: to persuade them to become children of God.

Certain churches are indifferent to evangelism because they christen babies, supposedly elevating them to Christian sonship. In these churches the phrase "born again" disappears, and all the minister preaches is reformation and growth. All they do is educate unregenerate people.

But when we are truly born again, it opens the door for God to use us. "And that ye put on the new man, which after God is created in righteousness and true holiness" (Eph. 4:24). We are to follow after Christ, discard old habits and ways of thinking, and walk before Him in newness of life, holy and righteous.

Perhaps you have attended church for years. You work for the church; you sing hymns; you fellowship with Christian people; you rejoice in the progress of the church. But in spite of all these motions you are not sure if you are a child of God. Why not be certain? Why pay every price that real Christians do and not be sure of your salvation? You may receive Jesus Christ as your Lord and Savior by believing on Him with all your heart and making public your profession of faith in Him. Christ stands with open arms, willing to welcome you into true sonship — and with it the eternal inheritance of the saints.

PART 2

THE PRACTICAL CHRISTIAN WALK

SIX

JESUS, MORE OR LESS

The law of cults and heresies

Most of us have answered a knock on our door and been faced with someone peddling a peculiar understanding of the Scriptures. I say peculiar because these solicitors have memorized certain Scripture portions that seem to make sense when put together with others and based upon certain premises.

We may not be able to detect their beliefs as false, because their theology will play upon our convictions. Almost imperceptibly we may find ourselves argued into a corner. Unless we have learned the Scriptures and the teaching of

God's Word in its entirety, we may feel that their beliefs make sense. We may even be tempted to join a heretical movement.

However, Scripture provides us with light that illumines the way cultists behave and enables us to separate the false from the true. The law of cults and heresies states: *The validity of all religious movements must be measured against the fullness of Christ.*

All Things Summed Up in Christ

What are the symptoms of these movements that should instantly put us on guard?

First, let's establish John 14:6 as a foundation: "Jesus saith unto him, I am the way, the truth, and the life: no man cometh unto the Father, but by me."

If Jesus Christ is the measurement of truth, if He is the Son of God, if He is to be the judge of the world, then everything has to be judged in the light of what He said, what He was and what He did. If we claim Jesus is not the truth of God, but merely another religious teacher such as Buddha, Zoroaster, Confucius or Mohammed, then He is no more than the founder of another religion. We have taken away His unique sonship.

As the only begotten Son of God, Jesus has a unique relationship to God: "I and my Father are one" (John 10:30). If Jesus and the Father are in oneness, then what Jesus said is what God said. But if Jesus was fooling Himself or us or was engaged in an ego trip because He fancied Himself a messiah, then He was a false teacher.

But Jesus was not mistaken. Everything He said stands up under the experience of the centuries. Everything He did and experienced in the Gospels, including miracles and His own resurrection, has withstood scholarly scrutiny and in some cases is supported by other sources. His life fulfills Old Testament prophecy with amazing detail.

Therefore if we believe Jesus Christ is the Son of God, and that Jesus and the Father are one, all teachings and everything else have to be judged by what He said, what He was and what He did. *Does a particular religious body agree with Jesus?* That's the issue. All cults and heresies hate the church, though they may not admit it. Cultists like to accept a smattering of Christianity, but they don't want all of it, so they simply choose those doctrines they want to incorporate into their theology.

Why Care About Cults?

Perhaps you have never been attracted to cultic teachings, and you wonder why you should be interested in this. It's because you're betting your life on Jesus if you're a Christian.

A day of severe testing of your faith may not have come yet, but it could, and you can't afford to be wrong when it does. When you believe Jesus is the Son of God, that Jesus and His Father are one, that He is *the* way, not one way, that He is *the* truth, not just a preacher of some truth, that only He is *the* life, then you will make all of your decisions in the light of that. That is betting your life on Jesus.

Furthermore, the responsibility for walking with integrity falls upon you as an individual, not on your church or denomination. Most Christians think they can accept passively what any Christian church, ministry or school dishes out, but that is not the case.

A man in San Francisco wrote me about a fund-raising letter he had received from a large women's religious college in another state, where he had enrolled his daughters. He had decided, before replying to the request for gifts, to visit the school. Upon arrival he found the sixteen hundred girls gathered for a Sunday morning service.

The first part of the service featured a dance whose theme was "God is dead!" One of the dancers, a "clergyman," had to keep changing his clerical garb because the old garments, symbolizing the traditional expression of God, were no longer suitable because God was dead. The task of the clergyman was to change costumes as he went from place to place, seeking ways to redefine God, because to most people God was dead.

A speaker then said, "The old religion is dead. God is dead. The old God is dead. Perhaps it is just as well. As we search for a new God — or God as we understand Him with our advanced understanding today — we find that the old morality based upon the old concept of God is dead too. From now on youth is going to have to find its way in redefining a new morality, because the old God is dead. So the new God will have to resemble the new concept of morality."

The speaker also said that sexual morality is changing. "It is no longer possible or sufficient to insist that premarital sex relations are wrong and evil in the sight of God. That God is dead, and from now on there will be an adjustment. We will have a new idea of God, and our God will not say, Is it wrong? He will ask, Is it *harmful*?"

In his letter of refusal to support this college with his gifts, my correspondent told the school administrators that he sent his daughters to that college instead of to his in-state schools, such as the University of California at Berkeley, because he thought they would be safer there. The service made it clear that such was not the case. He refused to give financial aid to this allegedly Christian school.

I find this thought reappearing continually today: the absurd idea that men can redefine God. God either exists or He does not. The whole concept of Christianity is that Jesus was the complete embodiment of God. God was "in Christ, reconciling the world unto himself" (2 Cor. 5:19). Yet you'll find this attempt to redefine God not only in radical cults but even in some places that use the label Christian.

Cults' Telltale Signs

All cults possess certain characteristics:

• They will always avoid teaching about the cross. No false cult ever exalts the crucified Savior. They may talk about His life. They may talk about His teachings. But they'll say very little about His crucifixion because that was the very purpose for which the Messiah was sent.

• It follows then that cults do not believe in the shed blood of Jesus as being sufficient for the remission of sins. Many cults fail even to acknowledge sin, writing it off as needless guilt that needs to be sloughed off.

• False cults will avoid talking about the bodily resurrection of Jesus. That irritates them. They're perfectly willing to talk about the persistence of personality beyond the grave, immortality of the soul — but the *bodily* resurrection? No.

Often ministers will preach on immortality at Easter. But immortality was believed in long before Easter. Easter is about the resurrection of the body, and that is quite different from immortality of the soul.

• Heretical cults and apostasies always exalt the self instead of the Savior. They emphasize selfishly: What can I get out of religion?

All this contradicts true Christianity, which does not tell us to come to church in order to feel good or gain a benefit. Meaningful sermons and enjoyable church activities are only part of what church is all about. Giving ourselves to Christ in service is the primary purpose of the local church.

One can cross from Christian immaturity to maturity in one short step. The line over which we tread is our decision to agree with Jesus, who said, "The son of man came not to be ministered unto, but to minister, and to give his life a ransom for many" (Mark 10:45). In contrast, cults and heresies exploit the fleshly desire to be ministered unto, then clothe their programs in religious garb.

Peter preached, "There is none other name under heaven given among men, whereby we must be saved" (Acts 4:12). Only when we exalt Jesus Christ to that exclusive place where God has placed Him are we able to gauge the degree to which cults and heresies and apostasies depart from Him.

Perverting the Faith

According to the U.S. Constitution, the government has no right to tell us how to worship. We regard that as a precious heritage. But we must not think that, in God's eyes, we have a right to worship Him as we see fit. There is a difference between a political right and intellectual integrity.

For example, I have the political right to bow down to the moon in worship and declare it is made of green cheese. But I don't have the intellectual right, because I know it is a dead ball of rock, not a dairy product. Yet if I tell my congregation I am worshipping the moon because it's made of cheese, I'm lying. I have violated my intellectual right.

All false cults, heresies and apostasies have the right to exist, and I would defend that political right as you would. But they do not have the intellectual right *if they claim to be Christian*. Some of their adherents admit they are not Christians. Others call themselves Christian, though they are not. They deceive because they claim to be something Jesus never modeled, the apostles never taught and the Bible does not mention.

For example, Methodists and Baptists belong to denominations — branches of Christianity. An individual Baptist or Methodist church might be apostate or heretical, though most are not. In the time of John Wesley or the early Baptists in America, church officials argued about baptism and various doctrines, but they were not heretical, because they did not depart from conformity to Jesus. They taught His Lordship.

A cult, however, can be a group of people who have

gathered out of a denomination because of disagreement with some fundamental teaching in Christianity. Many result from a heresy or an apostasy. Here is the difference between the two:

Heresy adds something to Christianity. A person may say, "I believe in the Bible, I believe in Jesus and I believe in the church, but I also believe in...," adding something that was never taught by Christ or the apostles — perhaps subtle worship of a charismatic leader or elevation of some ritual to the place of a divine mandate.

Apostasy takes something away from Christianity. It may be the authority of Scripture or perhaps some aspect of Christ's life — His virgin birth or His bodily resurrection. But the summation of an apostasy is something less than the entirety of the Bible's revealed truth.

One kind of heresy teaches that it is all right to be a Christian, but one also ought to be taught in certain mysteries that only a few people know. The early branch of that belief was called Gnosticism. The word comes from the Greek "to know," and it referred to those "who were in the know." It doesn't deny that Christ is the Son of God. It doesn't deny the Bible or any fundamental doctrines. It simply adds the belief that there are some secret teachings available only for the elite who listen to certain teachers.

This contradicts the biblical invitation, "And let him that is athirst come. And whosoever will, let him take the water of life freely" (Rev. 22:17). Christianity makes the truth available to everyone. Anyone who wants to come to Jesus must come as a little child, with no special education or privileges.

On the other hand, an apostate might declare, "I don't believe that Jesus is the Son of God. A good teacher, yes. A rabbi of unusual intelligence in the first century, yes. But I don't believe He died on the cross and shed His blood for our sins. I don't believe He was raised from the dead."

Many years ago I was acquainted with an associate pastor

of a congregation whose members prided themselves on being social and economic conservatives but religious liberals (no easy task). I asked one member what he believed.

"I don't believe in hell," he said.

"Fine," I said. "Tell me what you do believe in."

He replied, "I don't believe there is going to be a judgment."

"Fine," I said. "What do you believe?"

"I just can't see how a good God can sentence people to hell."

I wiped my brow in weariness. "Three times I have asked what you believe, and all you've told me is what you don't believe."

The members of the congregation never could tell me what they did believe because their faith was built upon what they didn't believe. They were guilty of apostasy. They believed in less than Christianity.

Rotten Tree, Rotten Fruit

The movements, or cults, that result from these heresies or apostasies all have one thing in common: advising their people to trust for salvation in a system of beliefs, an organization, a leader or one's own personal achievements — as well as in Jesus Christ. It says trust in Jesus, but also trust in keeping the Sabbath day or the Jewish law or not eating meat or not going to certain types of entertainment or going to certain places or having a certain feast or going without something or a thousand and one things that are not taught in the New Testament. Or it will say put your trust in Jesus — plus the exalted leader of our group.

Salvation is by faith through the grace of God (Eph. 2:8), and it is from Jesus Christ alone. By that truth we can test a teaching as false or not.

When somebody knocks on our door, inviting us to their church, we must find out what they believe. Do they trust in Christ alone for salvation? Do they trust in His shed blood, in His sacrificial work on the cross, in His deity, in His resurrection? Or do they trust in Christ, plus their good works, their religious ceremonies and their doctrines? That's a heresy, whether it's in a denominational church or not.

The same law holds true in apostasy, where the followers trust in something other than Christ for salvation. For example, a psychologist, in a letter to the editor of *Time* magazine, once accused Billy Graham of laying guilt on people. The psychologist claimed he spent all his time convincing people of their innocence. Not only did this man misunderstand Graham's message, but he didn't even understand good psychiatry, which acknowledges the reality of guilt. Graham preaches that we are guilty, but he is quick to add that Jesus Christ is a remedy for guilt.

We don't solve anybody's psychiatric problems by telling them they are not guilty when deep in their hearts they know they are. "For all have sinned, and come short of the glory of God" (Rom. 3:23). "There is none righteous, no, not one" (Rom. 3:10). If that's where the Bible ended, it would be a sorry book indeed. It continues, "For the wages of sin is death; but the gift of God is eternal life through Jesus Christ our Lord" (Rom. 6:23).

The apostate says, "Don't worry about believing in the shed blood of Jesus; it doesn't matter. If there's a God, He's quite grandfatherly, and He will let you by." The apostate fails to face the reality of sin, hell and judgment. He will never preach a sermon on Hebrews 9:27: "It is appointed unto men once to die, but after this the judgment." Instead, he will preach how we can overcome by new thinking or some other philosophy.

Don't come short of the revelation of God that was in Jesus. If God be God, serve Him. If Baal be God, serve him. But if you are convinced that Jesus is the Son of God, bet your life on Him. Don't settle for something that comes short of Him. As Part 2 of this book will show, Jesus has made a way for us to walk in success and personal fulfillment in every area of life. Apart from Him we will never know the fullness for which He created us.

SEVEN

THE LAWS
THAT LIBERATE

The law of the ten
New Testament commandments

Before changing clothes after Sunday school, the little boy rushed next door to find his friend.

"You won't believe what we learned in church today!" he told him breathlessly. "We had a lesson on the Ten *Commandos!*"

This young Bible student missed the point altogether, but no worse than thousands of more mature Christians have done. The Ten Commandments that God gave Moses express the moral will of God for ancient Israel and have become the platform for social morality in many lands.

Children memorize them. Most politicians speak approvingly about them. Even nonchurch people claim some kind of agreement with them. It is even popular to say that they are the foundation of our modern legal codes, though this is only partly true. American jurisprudence is based upon British law, which in turn came from ancient Roman law rather than Hebrew law.

Nevertheless, the influence of the Ten Commandments has been enormous. Though the religious commandments among the ten are ignored by modern society, the social commandments are hailed with respect, even though some are widely disobeyed.

This chapter will establish three things:

• The meaning of the Old Testament Ten Commandments and how they were fulfilled in Christ.

• Why they are not as relevant to Christians as the law of Christ.

• How the new covenant is expressed in the "new" Ten Commandments.

As we explore these aspects, we will come to understand the law of the ten New Testament commandments: *The Mosaic Ten Commandments were mostly intended to keep man from sin; New Testament commandments are meant to liberate man into the fullness of serving God with power.*

A Special Code for Israel

The *principles* of the Ten Commandments of Moses are universal, but the commandments as a legal code were intended more for Israel than for the world at large. This important truth is implied in Nehemiah 9:13-14, written about nine hundred years after the giving of the law: "Thou camest down also upon mount Sinai, and spakest with them from heaven, and gavest them right judgments, and true laws, good statutes and commandments: And madest known unto them thy holy sabbath, and commandedst them precepts, statutes, and laws, by the hand of Moses thy servant."

Therefore a full revelation of the Sabbath was not known until Mount Sinai (though a Sabbath observance is mentioned in Exodus 16, four chapters ahead of Mount Sinai). It could not be considered a universal law in the same sense that other universal moral truths, such as the prohibition of murder, were included in the Ten Commandments. Of the Sabbath, God said to Moses, "It is a sign between me and the children of Israel for ever" (Ex. 31:17). The principle of a holy day is good in all ages, as is the principle of regular rest, but the Sabbath commandment *as such* was for Israel alone. This shows how the entire code of the Ten Commandments is something less than a universal law.

A Higher Standard

Let us look at all of the Ten Commandments:

Thou shalt have no other gods before me.

Thou shalt not make unto thee any graven image, or any likeness of any thing that is in heaven above, or that is in the earth beneath, or that is in the water under the earth....

Thou shalt not take the name of the Lord thy God in vain; for the Lord will not hold him guiltless that taketh his name in vain.

Remember the sabbath day, to keep it holy.

Honour thy father and thy mother: that thy days may be long upon the land which the Lord thy God giveth thee.

Thou shalt not kill.

Thou shalt not commit adultery.

Thou shalt not steal.

Thou shalt not bear false witness against thy neighbour.

Thou shalt not covet thy neighbour's house, thou shalt not covet thy neighbour's wife, nor his manservant, nor his maidservant, nor his ox, nor his ass, nor any thing that is thy neighbour's (Ex. 20:3,4,7,8,12-17).

Christians are not under this law. Neither the ceremonial laws, the Ten Commandments, the entire Mosaic law or any other religious *law* reigns over Christians. The law was laid aside as the way of life for the Christians by Jesus Himself, as well as by the apostles. If you doubt this assertion, read the book of Galatians, especially Galatians 2:16; 3:10-14, 16-18, 24-26. Also consult Romans 3:21-27; 7:6; Hebrews 10:11-17, 38.

Some Christians are horrified at this thought. "Do you mean we can steal, bear false witness, take God's name in vain and murder?" This is *not* what I mean. It is not that the Ten Commandments were done away with. It is rather that *they were left behind as Christians climbed to a higher plane of relationship with Christ.*

We would be false to the New Testament if we taught that Christians are under the Ten Commandments. All Old Testament law was fulfilled in Christ. Now those laws are superseded by the new commandments in Christ.

For example, multiplication tables are useful, but higher mathematics goes beyond them to the glories of algebra and calculus. It is not that multiplication tables are abolished, but they are merely the beginning. As Paul wrote, the law is a "schoolmaster" to bring us to Christ (Gal. 3:24). We are no longer under the schoolmaster.

But there is more: Paul said, "He that loveth another hath fulfilled the law" (Rom. 13:8). In the next verse he repeats most of the Ten Commandments so we may see it is *not* only the ceremonial law but the Ten Commandments that have been outgrown by the new commandments rooted in love. Paul was paraphrasing Christ's words in Luke 10:24-37.

Of course, no Christian theologian argues against the idea that the ceremonial law was done away with. But there is much foolish argument that the moral law is still binding. Yet nowhere in the New Testament are the Ten Commandments presented as the primary moral standard for Christian living.

Moving Beyond Prohibitions

The Ten Commandments are restrictive, negative and confining. They say "Thou shalt not" in all but two commandments. They are designed to keep human nature in check, to thwart our natural inclinations. There is no *life* in them, no power to overcome anything. This is why Paul called them the law of sin and death. They are designed to keep people from sinning.

Avoiding sin is important but too elementary to be the final word. *We need power to overcome our natural impulses,* not mere restrictions against our fleshly or prideful nature.

When the law has revealed what sin is, it has fulfilled its purpose. It profoundly reveals that all have sinned — there is none righteous, not one! But the law cannot tell us what *to do*. It can only tell us what *not* to do and condemn us when we do wrong.

It remains for the mercy of God, as expressed and personified in Christ and His death on the cross, to demonstrate that there is forgiveness for the broken law. The function of the law is to show us our need for Christ to forgive and the Holy Spirit to empower us to live on a higher level than mere keeping of rules. Even if a person kept the law, it would be a passive righteousness, based on the things he did *not* do.

Righteousness that pleases God is usually active. It is established by what we do as well as what we refrain from doing. We are told never to take comfort in that we do not kill or do not deny that God exists. Real righteousness is in making people whole through love, in serving God through love, in exercising faith.

This is the kind of faith that was reckoned unto Abraham for righteousness. We make a grave mistake if we believe that people in Old Testament times were justified by keeping the law. As Romans 4:1-25 makes clear, they were justified by faith, just as we are today.

From Prison to Power

While Christians do not live by the Ten Commandments God gave to Moses, a careful reading of the New Testament will reveal a new set of Ten Commandments, almost unnoticed by most Christians, which have in them the full principles of Christianity.

Unlike the ten restrictive commandments of Mount Sinai, *these* commandments are full of power to help! They do not bind, but set free. They are not based upon "Thou shalt not" but are golden keys which unlock the doors of victory, blessing and deliverance. These commandments are found in 1 Thessalonians 5:11-22:

> Wherefore comfort yourselves together, and edify one another, even as also ye do. And we beseech you, brethren, to know them which labour among you, and are over you in the Lord, and admonish you; and to esteem them very highly in love for their work's sake. And be at peace among yourselves. Now [we] exhort you, brethren, warn them that are unruly, comfort the feebleminded, support the weak, be patient toward all men.
>
> See that none render evil for evil unto any man; but ever follow that which is good, both among yourselves, and to all men.
>
> Rejoice evermore.
>
> Pray without ceasing.
>
> In every thing give thanks: for this is the will of

God in Christ Jesus concerning you.
   Quench not the Spirit.
   Despise not prophesyings.
   Prove all things.
   Hold fast that which is good.
   Abstain from all appearance of evil.

Just as the original Ten Commandments were aimed at restricting the lower nature, the natural impulses of men in their relationships with man and God, these commandments *open up* the relationship of Christians with others and with their heavenly Father. Moreover, these commandments, if obeyed, do away with the need to worry about keeping the original ten.

Christianity was never meant to bind or shackle people. The new life in Christ is power, not imprisonment! It sets men free to become what they are intended to be in Christ.

We should never give young people the impression that church attendance, Bible reading and Christianity exist only to make them good, and therefore they should refrain from doing all sorts of things that break the law of God. As surely as we do, we give them the impression that Christianity is only the modern equivalent of the Ten Commandments of Israel.

We should instead teach them that Christianity is liberation from the enslavement of sin. The world — cruel, heartless, ruled by satanic forces — is trying to enslave people in its lusts, passions, false standards, fads and opinions, and make them dance to its tune. Christ wants to set them free from sin and death and release in them His mighty power so that they may overcome themselves and the siren song of the world. No one is ashamed of power. And that is what Christianity is — power!

Power Pack

Let us see how the Christian Ten Commandments assist us to release in ourselves the power of God:

1. *Edify one another.* "Edify" is an old-fashioned word that means "to build up." We are not to tear other people down by cruel, cutting remarks or actions. Instead we are to be known as the people who build up everyone we meet. We believe when others doubt. We forgive when others hold unforgiveness.

This commitment to edify others would automatically keep one away from many sins prohibited by the original Ten Commandments, such as theft, murder, envy or covetousness.

2. *See that none render evil for evil, but follow that which is good.* This directly contrasts with the Mosaic law of "an eye for an eye." The Lord Jesus said we were not to seek vengeance but to forgive, again and again if need be. To pay back evil for evil is human, but Christians are to be superhuman, in a sense, because they have a supernatural God within them. Besides, they have an awareness of how much *they* have been forgiven and how little they deserve it.

3. *Rejoice evermore.* Real joy is more than happiness or pleasure. It is a deep sense of well-being that comes from knowing who we are and to whom we belong. We know who we are from our relationships. A person who does not *know* who he is is a person who doesn't *belong* to something or someone outside himself.

We have the privilege of belonging to the church as a great cause, to God as the supreme Person and to each other as brethren in Christ. This gives us identity and deep strength, resulting in joy. True joy motivates us to rejoice evermore in spite of suffering, privation, betrayal, misunderstanding and sorrow. Imagine — a command to rejoice!

4. *Pray without ceasing.* This does not mean without stopping. It means not to give up in prayer. You could translate

the Greek as being "stretched-outedly" in prayer. Don't give up praying until the answer comes or you have the assurance in your heart that the answer is on the way. This is one of the brightest of the Christian's Ten Commandments.

5. *In everything give thanks.* The attitude of the truly grateful heart is thanksgiving due to the realization that all things have come through grace. Only the person who doesn't know what grace is, or the person who thinks he is personally responsible for his own accomplishments and prosperity, feels no need to be thankful. How much selfishness and godlessness could be avoided with a continual attitude of thanksgiving!

It's easy to be thankful for happy conditions. But this commandment says to be thankful in *every* circumstance.

6. *Quench not the Spirit.* Are you a spiritual wet blanket? Are you always holding back when the Holy Spirit wants you or the church to move ahead? You can grieve the Holy Spirit by sin or quench Him by a lack of faith. Unwillingness to "launch out into the deep" is often to blame for the powerlessness and poverty of Christians. If you stay in the shallows, your reward will be shallow. You will be shallow too.

7. *Despise not prophesyings.* To prophesy, as the New Testament writers used the word, was to preach with warning. It was not so much prediction as to preach about the inevitability of certain types of conduct. "The soul that sinneth, it shall die" (Ezek. 18:20) is prophecy of this type. This New Testament commandment exhorts us not to take such warnings lightly.

8. *Test everything.* Prove all things to see what will hold up under a strain. Too many allurements look like diamonds but are only glass.

Benjamin Franklin, as a lad, dumped a handful of coins on the counter of the village store.

"Will this buy that whistle?" he asked.

"Of course," said the clerk.

Franklin later learned he could have had the whistle for only one penny. He never forgot that he paid too much for the whistle, which soon fell apart.

In the same way we are paying too much for some desirable things which, like the whistle, make only a shrill noise and don't last. And I don't mean simply wasting money on frivolous items at the store. We become more spiritually bankrupt whenever we deviate from God's will. Truly, the wages of sin are death, both on earth and after we die. No one would break any moral law if he could see how poorly sin pays off. Yet the nature of temptation is that it looks on the surface to be highly desirable. We must test all things.

9. *Hold fast that which is good*. The world is full of stories of people who traded property which was later found to have enormous wealth buried in it or was about to become extremely valuable for development.

Too easily we trade our convictions and our spiritual gains for something novel that has not stood the test of time. Our times are changing at a fearful rate. The *rate* of change even more than the *fact* of change is one of the dominant forces of our age. Unlike previous generations, the world into which we were born has already been completely transformed. The world in which our children will live is not yet here.

Scripture says the shaking is taking place so the things that cannot be shaken may remain. Those things — those eternal truths — are what we must cling to.

10. *Abstain from every form of evil*. Not "appearance of evil," which is a widely accepted mistranslation. The Greek word means not the *look* of evil, but *every shape* of evil. The Christian is to be good in his innermost being, his thoughts and his conscience, as well as appearing beyond reproach to the unsaved as he conducts his life.

True Liberation

Amid these Ten Commandments there appears the phrase "for this is the will of God in Christ Jesus concerning you." When a true Christian gets his marching orders from God, that is enough. Are you seeking the will of God for your life? Well, here it is.

What a liberating force these commandments are! Not restricting and binding life, or keeping a close rein over our basic inclinations, but setting us free to be what God has purposed us *to be*.

As Paul concluded, however, even these power-filled commandments cannot be obeyed by mere willpower. To *wish* to do good is ever present with us. To *perform* that which we sincerely *intend* when we promise to obey is another thing. So Paul adds, "Faithful is he that calleth you, who also will do it" (1 Thess. 5:24). Even when we fail, He fails not. "If we confess our sins [failures], he is faithful and just to forgive us our sins, and to cleanse us from all unrighteousness" (1 John 1:9).

So don't struggle to fulfill these commandments. Be receptive of God's grace. Let Him work His will and good pleasure in you!

EIGHT

SOW WHAT?

The law of consequences

A narchist Jerry Rubin, urging young people to forsake their responsibilities and become revolutionaries, said don't study history; *make* history.

Too many students agree with this fast-food philosophy. The results are tragic and chaotic. Those who do not know where they are going inevitably go *wrong*! Not one person in any prison ever arrived there who did not first ignore the full consequences of his decisions.

One attribute of maturity that youths often lack is an *awareness of consequences*. How could it be otherwise? How could we expect young people, who have not had many of life's transforming experiences, to be aware of what the consequences of their every decision will be? That kind of understanding comes only by experience and learning.

Even logical thinking cannot totally reveal probable consequences. That's because logic is based on man's rationale, and that does not always line up with God's wisdom. Besides, humans are not primarily creatures of logic. We often suppose we reason when what we actually do is feel. Emotions often blind us so that we cannot see what is coming. Our strong feelings demand satisfaction now — not tomorrow, not after a long period of self-discipline, but *now*! Emotions, therefore, are unsafe guides for youth in times of decision-making. It is through the glory and crown of age that one learns to be aware of consequences.

A person unconcerned about consequences will not plot a path toward goals, nor could he follow that path even if he did set certain objectives. He will drift and never realize until it is too late that failing to decide is in itself a decision.

Is there a sure prescription for failure? Act as if there were no such thing as a consequence, and you will fail every time. Live for the moment. Have no awareness that the seeds you sow today will bring a harvest tomorrow, whether for good or ill. Failure will come swiftly.

The law of consequences — *we will reap what we sow* — is the greatest law for living there is. It is the wise man who knows what consequences mean and who is able to predict them and to discipline his life by this knowledge as he achieves his goals.

Building for the Storm

Jesus said:

> Whosoever cometh to me, and heareth my sayings, and doeth them, I will shew you to whom he

is like: He is like a man which built an house, and digged deep, and laid the foundation on a rock: and when the flood arose, the stream beat vehemently upon that house, and could not shake it: for it was founded upon a rock. But he that heareth, and doeth not, is like a man that without a foundation built an house upon the earth; against which the stream did beat vehemently, and immediately it fell; and the ruin of that house was great (Luke 6:47-49).

What is the outcome of building upon sand versus building upon rock? Inevitable, inexorable consequences! You may construct the same house, but what is the ultimate difference? It is the destiny of the house, determined when the builder makes his choices. The wise builder looks into the future and sees the stormy weather beating upon his foundation. Because he is aware of consequences, he knows how the sand is going to react and how the rock is going to react. So *he* builds his house upon the rock.

People come to Christ in different ways, but many come by first looking at the consequences of their life choices. For example, you might ask, Who am I? Upon meditation, you realize: I am an immortal soul, made in the image of God. I am not merely a biological being, but a human being made in the image of the divine Being. I have a spiritual destiny. A million years from now I will be somewhere.

You then reflect: Yet I realize that God is holy, and I am sinful. If I persist in saying "no, no, no" to God, the time will come when God will say "no, no, no" to me. Lest that fearful time come, I must make my peace with God *now*.

These steps of reasoning are based upon an awareness of consequences. One should consider the consequences of becoming a Christian — and vice versa. Jesus urged that no person become a Christian until he first looks at the consequences.

The Bible calls this "counting the cost." Jesus illustrated that truth: "And a certain scribe came, and said unto him, Master, I will follow thee whithersoever thou goest. And Jesus saith unto him, The foxes have holes, and the birds of the air have nests; but the Son of man hath not where to lay his head" (Matt. 8:19-20).

The man had said to Jesus, "I want to become one of your disciples! I want to enroll in your school."

"Come ahead," said Jesus, "but first be reminded of the consequences of your decision." Jesus never pulled the wool over anyone's eyes. "Before you follow Me, *count the cost*. There *is* a price that has to be paid. Don't try to follow Me unless you are ready to pay it!"

Jesus did not overemphasize the cost because that would have made His way seem one of self-punishment. Neither did He underemphasize it. He simply requires people to consider it.

Consequences and Your Future

Because Christianity is concerned with consequences, you might expect it to prophesy about the future. Not surprisingly, one-third of the Bible *is* prophecy. How could it be otherwise? A faith based upon an awareness of consequences must have foresight. Foresight and wisdom should be revealed in prophecy — and so they are.

Do not think of prophecy as something occultic, unscientific or unsophisticated in this "learned" age. The prophecies of the Scriptures are the natural outflow of the very nature of God's heart to guide His people.

Many of the prophecies tend to echo the law of consequences: "The soul that sinneth, it shall die" (Ezek. 18:4). "Whatsoever a man soweth, that shall he also reap" (Gal. 6:7). Prophecy is heaped upon prophecy in the Scriptures!

The Bible foretells what is going to happen to nations, to churches, to individuals, to you. The consequences it plainly predicts for each of us can therefore assist us in choosing the path we should take.

Why did the Son of God spell out so clearly for us the final results of disobedience as well as the rewards of obedience? Because out of His heart of love He would have us look ahead that we might choose the path that leads to joy, not sorrow. He affirmed: "These things have I spoken unto you, that my joy might remain in you, and that your joy might be full" (John 15:11).

The Bible never fails to set out for us the results of men's foolish ways. In case history after case history in God's great record book of human behavior, we are shown how people have always suffered the penalty and effects of their self-willed actions and choices.

Eve thought she might eat of the forbidden fruit and have godlike knowledge of good and evil, but because of her disobedience she and Adam were evicted from the Garden of Eden. David lusted after Bathsheba, and his unchecked sin resulted in adultery, murder and the death of an infant. All of mankind except for Noah's family was drowned because they chose to live unrighteously. Cause and effect follow each other as surely as night follows day, from generation to generation, forever.

No Exceptions

These examples and others throughout God's Word reflect the sad story of people who thought they could be an exception to God's laws. Even today the man who steals is determined to prove that the admonition "your sin will find you out" does not apply to him. The man who works seven days a week, fifty-two weeks a year, without serving God is attempting to show that "six days shalt thou labor" was not commanded for such an exceptional man as he. Mankind relentlessly tries to disprove God's principle that we reap what we sow. But in vain!

Concerning the inevitability of consequences, Ralph Waldo Emerson, in his essay "Compensation," observed:

> This Law writes the laws of cities and nations....
>
> Life invests itself with inevitable conditions, which the unwise seek to dodge.... If he escapes them in one part, they attack him in another more vital part. If he has escaped them in form, and in appearance, it is because he has resisted his life, and fled from himself, and the retribution is so much death.
>
> All things are double, one against another. —Tit for tat; an eye for an eye.... —Give and it shall be given you. —He that watereth shall be watered himself. —What will you have? quoth God; pay for it and take it.... —It is thus written, because it is thus in life.[1]

For this reason Christians of all people should be those who live not only for *today* but for *tomorrow*; for they *know* what tomorrow will bring. Christians need not worry about the future as others do. They know that even when life's path temporarily goes underground into the grave, it emerges on the other side as a consequence of their decision to surrender to God now.

It is this eternity-awareness that gives Christianity the ability to help its followers to understand who they are and where they are going. Real Christians have an awareness of their destiny and purpose. They do not wander aimlessly as others, who have no compass, who do not know how things are going to come out in the end.

Jesus cautioned the bigoted and blind Pharisees of His day, saying, in effect:

You stand at the top of cultured society. Scholastically, you have the best education of anyone these days, and in *natural* things you are very wise. For example, in the afternoon, when the sky is red, you rightly say, "Tomorrow will be a fair day." When the morning sky is red, you say, "The consequences of this portend a foul day." Oh, you hypocrites! You can so wisely analyze the face of the sky and read its signs, *but you cannot read the signs of the times!*

He accused them of being cultural sophisticates and spiritual idiots. They could not see the important spiritual consequences of their decisions.

Changing Times

Notice how the Sermon on the Mount is imbued with this philosophy. Jesus was saying: Look ahead at the consequences of your choices. Count the cost of giving your attention to earthly things alone.

What did He mean? What is the one constant fact about earth? *That nothing is constant.* The only thing changeless about earth is that everything is changing. The mountains are slowly eroding; the seas evaporate, and their shorelines move; men are born, they mature and they die; old institutions crumble; old landmarks are torn down.

Look at the consequences of constant change, Jesus warned: "Lay not up for yourselves treasures upon earth, where moth and rust doth corrupt, and where thieves break through and steal: But lay up for yourselves treasures in heaven, where neither moth nor rust doth corrupt, and where thieves do not break through nor steal: For where your treasure is, there will your heart be also" (Matt. 6:19-21).

How do your decisions match with what Jesus said?

Many individuals make decisions each day that ignore the dire consequences of choosing a wholly materialistic life, a life from which they must soon depart. Why then are so many people engrossed in material things? Because they are not wise. A wise man is one who has a sense of values, and he is aware of the penalties of ignoring proper priorities and consequences in his choices.

If you are in trouble and call for a wise man, whom will you find? He will be the person with the foresight to guide you out of your difficulty. This foresight will be based upon hindsight and insight — wisdom gained by realizing that every decision we make inevitably brings consequences.

This is the lesson of history, the lesson of the future and the lesson of wisdom. You have only one life, and it is soon over. Why misdirect it? Begin now to weigh the fruit of every decision. As we will see next, this approach is imperative to achieving success yet is challenging to maintain because evil has an inherent advantage over righteousness in terms of consequences.

---

1. Ralph Waldo Emerson, "Compensation," as quoted in *Ralph Waldo Emerson: Essays and Lectures* (New York: Library of America, 1983), pp. 285-302.

NINE

WILLING TO WAIT

The law of good and evil

A member of my former church in Fort Worth, Texas, sought me for counseling many years ago.

"I don't behave very well in church," he said. "I don't always do things right. I don't always handle people well. I've had three jobs during the six months you've been here as pastor. I can't hold a job. I don't know what's the matter with me."

As he delved into his past, he confessed that he had contracted syphilis when he was young. At the time we spoke I was studying for a doctorate in psychology and was serving in a hospital as an orderly and intern in the field of psychosomatics. I had studied the effects of syphilis.

I couldn't muster the courage to tell him that although his syphilis had been cured, it had not been cured quickly enough; the spinal fluids and brain had been affected. His behavior was the result of a hardening of the arteries of the brain. I didn't have the heart to tell him the day would come when he would imagine flies crawling over his face, and he would be constantly slapping at them. Eventually he would sit in a corner and stare.

That man was to suffer a lifetime of terrible consequences for his moment of pleasure. He would experience the downside of what the last chapter showed to be the law of consequences: *We reap what we sow.*

Christians frequently put a bad connotation on Galatians 6:7: "Whatsoever a man soweth, that shall he also reap." We are quick to think how, if we sow sin, we will reap sin and its fruits. However, it is just as true that we can sow righteousness and reap the fruits of righteousness. There is one key difference, though: *Good must be paid for first and enjoyed later. Evil can be enjoyed now but has to be paid for later.* That is the law of good and evil.

Prepared for Your Place

The Bible presents two alternatives: Whatever we choose to take, we will pay for — sooner (in the case of good) or later (in the case of evil). But in either case we pay for our choices.

Getting a good education, for example, is a pretty painful process, but those who plow through the years of study, paying the price first, will enjoy forever the fruits of it. For instance, the earning power of a person who receives a college education rises dramatically through life. The more we sacrifice to gain an education in early life, the further we go, even though we may have had to postpone things we would have loved to do. The hard work pays off.

Years ago I attended a Bible institute whose motto was "God has prepared places for prepared people." Not just in ministry, but in every realm, life has not prepared places for everybody, but only for those who are prepared. Jesus urged His followers to be faithful over a few things so that the Father would make them rulers over many (Matt. 25:23). It's applicable in the army — if we're faithful over a small task, we're promoted to a larger task. In the business world, those who handle well a small responsibility will be trusted with a larger one. And when Jesus comes again, those who have been faithful in a few things will be made ruler over many.

A Hell of a Vacation

The real rewards, and therefore the key to happiness in life, lie in this. The better job we do, the more we are rewarded with greater responsibility. Some would complain, "That's no great reward. I'm looking forward to getting out of work, not gaining more responsibility." But that attitude shows a lack of wisdom. Nobody is more miserable than the person who is no longer harnessed to something he was born to do.

A wicked man died and found himself in a sumptuous palace. A servant knocked on the door, handed him his breakfast and said, "There's an eighteen-hole golf course here for you and a swimming pool. Just make yourself right at home." Day after day he enjoyed his fill of luxury. But in two or three weeks he grew tired of it and inquired of the butler, "Isn't there something I can work at around here? I'm tired of doing nothing."

"Oh, no," replied the butler. "There's not a thing to do here. Just enjoy yourself."

"Well," the man murmured, "I thought that when I died and went to heaven I'd enjoy myself, but I'm getting tired of this. I never thought I'd get tired of heaven. Sometimes I think I would rather have gone to hell!"

The butler peered at him. "Sir, just *where* do you think you *are*?"

Of course, the Bible makes it clear that hell is a place of punishment, so those hellbound can expect to face something worse than a perpetual resort vacation. But it's easily imaginable that part of that punishment will be the stunning awareness that one will be eternally useless.

The Strength of Evil

The law of good and evil applies universally. For example, we must take care of the body — often paying the price of inconvenient exercise or a diet that we find unappealing — if we are to enjoy health throughout most of our lives.

It's true in salvation. To be eligible for salvation — divine sonship, having Christ as our companion, God as our Father and heaven our home — a price must first be paid. Buddha didn't die to ransom anybody. Mohammed didn't die to ransom anybody. But Jesus did so on the cross.

Why? Because the cost has to be met first, and then the good can be enjoyed forever. Evil is stronger than good *temporarily* because the pleasure can be enjoyed immediately. This is the strength of evil.

It only takes a split second to decide to reap the fruits of evil. Nobody needs to count pennies all his life in hope of some day becoming a bank robber. Instead, he robs a bank now so he can enjoy the fruits of it immediately.

The strength of evil's attraction becomes clear in the Bible's opening pages:

> But of the fruit of the tree which is in the midst of the garden, God hath said, Ye shall not eat of it, neither shall ye touch it, lest ye die.... For God doth know that in the day ye eat thereof, then your eyes shall be opened, and ye shall be as gods, knowing

> good and evil. And when the woman saw that the
> tree was good for food, and that it was pleasant to
> the eyes, and a tree to be desired to make one wise,
> she took of the fruit thereof, and did eat, and gave
> also unto her husband with her; and he did eat
> (Gen. 3:3, 5-6).

The attraction of evil is its capacity for immediate enjoyment, as Adam and Eve discovered. I am sure the apple was as delicious as they thought it would be. But their action was followed by a lifetime of misery.

Herein is also evil's deception. Satan says, "Don't worry about the consequences of your choices. Do what you want. Be yourself. Don't worry about tomorrow. Don't prepare. Live it up."

That's deceiving. The fruits of evil are ever ripening, though the process may take years to manifest itself.

We can see the lure of the present operating in socialistic countries and even in some democracies where there are strong demands for the government to provide an endless list of needs and wants, from prenatal care to our daily bread to retirement benefits — no matter what the cost. Such developments are driven by a public attitude of: Enjoy now — the government will take care of the future. Prolonged dependency on this sort of system can only weaken individual and family responsibilities to care for self and others. The results in some countries have been stagnating economies and family disintegration, evidenced by high rates of divorce, illegitimate births and cohabitation.

This attitude of demanding certain provisions *now*, no matter who has to pay for them, violates a basic law of God's kingdom:

> Go to the ant, thou sluggard; consider her ways,
> and be wise: which having no guide, overseer, or
> ruler, provideth her meat in the summer, and

gathereth her food in the harvest. How long wilt thou sleep, O sluggard? when wilt thou arise out of thy sleep? Yet a little sleep, a little slumber, a little folding of the hands to sleep: so shall thy poverty come as one that travelleth, and thy want as an armed man (Prov. 6:6-11).

Advance planning and work bring prosperity. Procrastination, or dependence on someone else to meet needs, yields the opposite. You cannot escape the law of good and evil.

Window of Opportunity

I once stood over a grave with a husband as he laid a wreath of flowers upon the grave. Through his tears he murmured, "It is the greatest regret of my life that these are the first flowers I ever gave my wife."

What happened to him? He had forgotten there is a time limit for our actions on earth. The Bible exhorts us, "Remember now thy Creator in the days of thy youth, while the evil days come not, nor the years draw nigh, when thou shalt say, I have no pleasure in them" (Eccl. 12:1).

A time factor is attached to all good and evil. "Today if ye will hear his voice, harden not your hearts" (Heb. 3:15). Good has a time clause attached to it, just as an airline may offer a discount for those flying within a thirty-day period.

Eighty-five percent of Christians accepted Christ before the age of twenty. Beyond that age the percentage drops considerably. It's the old law at work. Those who refuse God's will and choose to cling to the evil ways of the flesh will be less receptive to the gospel as life goes on. Consequently, they may never get around to accepting Christ. And even if they do, they will regret having wasted those years they could have spent serving the Lord, storing up treasures in heaven.

Use It or Lose It

How does a farmer grow a good crop? He must work, sweat, plow, plant, cultivate and water. Afterward, having paid the price, he will reap the harvest. But if he doesn't plant and cultivate, or if he neglects his field, it will degenerate into a big weed patch.

Any good which is neglected always degenerates into an evil. Use it up or lose it. For any good that you have — a gift, a talent, an opportunity, a loved one — there's a time factor for how long it remains good. Any good neglected becomes an evil sooner or later.

But note the contrary: An evil neglected does not degenerate, does not become less evil. Left alone, evil always flourishes. *A little evil becomes a big one.* A temporary bad habit unchecked will naturally grow into a permanent one. A small attitude of selfishness becomes towering pride.

The Bible sums up this process: "To him that knoweth to do good, and doeth it not, to him it is sin" (James 4:17). That's because good degenerates into evil when it's neglected. As opportunity passes by, it closes doors. But as evil passes by unaddressed, it spreads. Mother, if you have an unruly child and leave him alone, he'll become an unruly adult. We don't have to train him to steal and to lie, to be deceptive, selfish and evil. But we do have to teach a child to be good, because the law of good and evil is at work everywhere. Jesus said to work now because the night is coming, when no man can work (John 9:4). The time clause is always present in matters of good and evil.

TEN

GUARDING THE INNER MAN

The law of inward failure

When the prophet Daniel arrived in Babylon as a hostage, he decided he didn't want any part of the immorality, idolatry and hedonism of the king's court.

He also rejected the king's food, being a devout Jew who observed the laws of kosher. One day the king's dietician insisted that Daniel and his friends eat the delicacies the king ordered for them. It would be interpreted as rebellion if they did not.

But Daniel purposed in his heart that he would not defile himself with the portion of the king's meat, nor with the wine which he drank: therefore he requested of the prince of the eunuchs that he might not defile himself (Dan. 1:8).

Daniel experienced astounding miracles and a life of success. He wrote one of the most notable books of the Old Testament. He was used of God to sustain the people of Israel. He embodied spiritual strength and became the prime minister under three or four Babylonian kings. Can we trace the source of his greatness? *"Daniel purposed in his heart."* He succeeded outwardly because he first succeeded inwardly.

Would you like to understand past failures? How about preventing future failures? Then learn the law of inward failure: *No man fails outwardly unless he first fails inwardly.* By the same token, to succeed outwardly we must first succeed inwardly.

Start With the Heart

The Bible emphasizes beginning with the inner man, or the heart. Rather than trying to change circumstances, the Bible commands us to change ourselves first — or more accurately, to let God do it.

Reinhold Niebuhr, a Christian professor of theology and a socialist, wrote an influential book titled *Moral Man and Immoral Society*. He argued that man is essentially good; it is only society that is immoral. In order to right all social wrongs, turn society toward socialism, and all will be well, for man really intends good.

Yet Jeremiah 17:9 says the heart of man is "deceitful above all things, and desperately wicked." One would think a professing Christian theologian would know that oft-recited passage. Niebuhr may have. He just didn't believe it.

"Keep thy heart with all diligence; for out of it are the issues of life" (Prov. 4:23). In other words, work hard at guarding your heart; your troubles begin not in your environment, but in yourself.

Defense attorneys have been known to plead, "This poor boy really never had a chance. It's true he committed a terrible crime, but after all, he came from a deprived neighborhood (or from a racial minority). And with all those strikes against him, you can't blame him for having turned out the way he did."

What the attorney fails to point out is that in the same ghetto lived other young men from broken homes who had the same poverty, the same lack of education, the same street gangs to entice them — but they grew up to be responsible citizens. Environmental circumstances can affect people, but to blame everything on such factors and ignore what goes on in the inner man falls far short of reality.

Expecting to solve problems only by changing society takes all the responsibility off the individual and puts it on the politicians. It puts it on economists. It blames anything that goes wrong on the system. *The Bible says we are to blame.* Individuals are accountable.

We can't have it both ways. Problems either start in society and overwhelm individuals, or problems begin in individual hearts and simply manifest themselves in society.

Jesus told a multitude, "Hear, and understand: Not that which goeth into the mouth defileth a man; but that which cometh out of the mouth, this defileth a man" (Matt. 15:10-11). The mouth speaks what it first finds in the heart. The Jews held to Mosaic law, which said they could be defiled by what they ate. But Jesus went on to elaborate on true defilement: "For out of the heart proceed evil thoughts, murders, adulteries, fornications, thefts, false witness, blasphemies: These are the things which defile a man: but to eat with unwashen hands defileth not a man" (Matt. 15:19-20).

The Heart Manifests Itself

The heart also affects behavior. "For as he thinketh in his heart, so is he" (Prov. 23:7). If a man thinks failure, he will be a failure. If he thinks success, he will be successful. If he thinks in terms of power, he may get power. We are the product of what we think. But if he thinks anything in a self-seeking way, he will use the outcome in a wrong way. The man who fails outwardly will have first failed inwardly, in his thought life.

What did Jesus have to say about our daily conversation? "A good man out of the good treasure of his heart bringeth forth that which is good; and an evil man out of the evil treasure of his heart bringeth forth that which is evil: for of the abundance of the heart his mouth speaketh" (Luke 6:45).

What do you speak about all the time? These are the subjects that are dearest to your heart.

Dwelling upon virtuous and good thoughts is one of the paths to success. A wealthy British publisher, Lord Beaverbrook, wrote a book about getting rich. He said that anyone can become rich beyond his fondest dreams, but it requires one thing: to think, eat, drink and talk money.

Beaverbrook was right. But that doesn't mean his advice should be followed.

Jesus said a man's life consists not in the abundance of things that he possesses. He asked how a rich man could enter the kingdom of heaven. Why should riches pose a problem? Not because they're evil, but because riches have a habit of crowding more worthy matters out of our minds. A man who thinks about money all the time often will become adept at making money. But he probably will pay the price of failing in his soul. And what shall it profit a man if he gain the whole world and lose his own soul?

In finding resources to face life, we are given a clear direction from Christ: "Let not your heart be troubled: ye believe in God, believe also in me" (John 14:1). Those who

94

are seeking resources to face life must first change their heart; then their outward circumstances can be changed and dealt with successfully.

What is your heart troubled about? Your job, security, health, family, finances, old age, our country? Put trouble away from your heart and resolve, I won't have it. But beware. Telling yourself that you don't have a problem, that you shouldn't feel discouraged, that things will work out, is an empty exercise by itself. The full approach to refusing trouble in our hearts involves trusting our loving Savior, who makes God and all His resources available to us.

The Role of Repentance

Realizing we can't blame our failures on God, our environment or other people helps us to see clearly that we alone are responsible for our failures, and we need salvation. Yet a man must respond to God's offer of salvation. That means repentance through faith in Christ.

Repentance is far more than feeling sorry for our sins, though it includes that. The Greek word for it means "to change the mind." That's why the forgiven person will confess, "I used to love sin, but now I hate it." Another may admit, "I used to place a high priority on the praise of society, but now I place a high priority on the praise of God." Another way of defining repentance is that it involves looking at life as God sees it.

Jesus contrasted two praying men — the Pharisee and the confessing publican. The rich man stood on high, praying, "God, I thank thee, that I am not as other men are, extortioners, unjust, adulterers, or even as this publican. I fast twice in the week, I give tithes of all that I possess" (Luke 18:11-12). He wanted God to understand that he was a good old boy. Because he was a good Jew, probably staying away from pork and keeping his beard cut according to the law, he felt he was justified. He showed no awareness of his pride. He needed to repent.

The publican bowed his head in the presence of God, crying, "God be merciful to me a sinner" (Luke 18:13). He had repented. He recognized his personal responsibilities for his mistakes. He had begun to realize the law of inward failure that is woven through the fabric of life.

The Same Yesterday and Today

How do we live a victorious Christian life? This was one of Paul's recipes:

> Servants, be obedient to them that are your masters according to the flesh, with fear and trembling, in singleness of your heart, as unto Christ; not with eyeservice, as menpleasers; but as the servants of Christ, doing the will of God from the heart" (Eph. 6:5-6).

To do the Lord's will from the heart. Sounds simple enough, doesn't it? After all, many people talk about the will of God. They go through the motions. They outwardly observe the laws, wanting to prove they are completely within God's will.

Jesus encountered a group of people like that — the Pharisees. Outwardly they were most religious. They tried to follow all the Mosaic law as well as their interpretations of that law. They didn't cut their robes beyond a certain length. They let their hair grow.

On one of my trips to Israel I drove into a neighborhood where a sect of modern-day Pharisees live. A man had told me to park the car before I reached the neighborhood. I thought he was mistaken.

So I drove into the neighborhood, and suddenly a huge rock bounced off my windshield. A little mob of Pharisees had gathered because I drove a car on the Sabbath, violating their interpretation of sabbath rest. They planned to demolish that car and apparently wouldn't have minded hitting me on the head. I escaped with only a cracked windshield.

All this had happened in the name of keeping the Sabbath. The Bible gives it another name: Phariseeism. This mind-set, unfortunately, is still with Christians. Often we can excel on the externals, being fine Christian Pharisees. But the secret of a victorious Christian life lies elsewhere: *Doing the will of God from the heart.*

Frequently a man will fail inwardly, and it won't be immediately apparent because the momentum of his right thinking and right decisions will carry him along. His inward failure won't manifest itself for a month, or six months, or a year. But in the end it will be apparent for all to see.

No tree ever toppled under a slight wind if its inner core was sound. But when a tree falls with a great crash, be assured that long ago the inner core began to rot.

We must guard our inner man. Hence, we are accountable to turn failures into successes by allowing God to change the inner man. If we yield to Him in repentance and exercise faith in His power to change us, He will be faithful to do so. We can sow seeds of success rather than seeds of failure in the inner man — and be confident of a glorious harvest.

One major key to keeping our inner man strong is maintaining a healthy prayer life. As the next three chapters will show, God has equipped us to tear down the things blocking our prayer life and has granted us the keys to effective prayer.

ELEVEN

GETTING GOD TO RETURN YOUR CALLS

The law of successful praying

Here's a brain teaser for you: Is life mainly pain occasionally relieved by pleasure? Or is it pleasure rudely interrupted by occasional pain?

Perhaps it is neither. Maybe both pain and pleasure merely disrupt our ordinary existence, which is a monotonous well-being.

Is it possible, then, to have a truly pleasurable life, virtually free from pain and disappointment? Many people try on their own to create such circumstances. They strive to accumulate money, to spread their own fame, to acquire vast material goods.

Yet Scripture makes plain that the good life depends not upon money, possessions or popularity. These have only a passing value. The more one has of each of these, beyond a certain modest level of adequacy, the greater the multiplication of responsibility and concern. Too great an increase of these falsely popular achievements can bring so many problems as actually to diminish the likelihood of the good life. For example, the possibility that you might lose certain valued objects by theft, or that your coveted recognition might suddenly be tarnished by some fickle incident beyond your control, can create terror.

Therefore the truly good life must be based upon that which is rooted in eternity, not that which is subject to change or decay. First Corinthians 13:13 points us in the direction of these eternal building blocks: "And now abideth faith, hope, charity." Faith produces peace. Hope produces joy. Charity produces love. The chief elements of the good life are peace, joy and love.

No one but God can bestow the three root "cardinal virtues." Where is faith in an age whose chief hallmark is unbelief? Where is hope in nature, which decrees that all must wither and die? Where is charity in society, which is selfish and cares only for its own?

Faith, hope and charity come from the good hand of the Father in response to prayer. Prayer, therefore, is the key to the good life. If we walk only in prayerless paths during this present life, we cannot expect to know the sweet gifts of God reserved for those who insert the keys of prayer and humbly enter the sanctuary.

Prayers That Work

If we dared note the actual time we give to prayer, we would be shocked. Besides that, our prayers themselves are so routine we often say them without actual thought. They too often follow the same familiar wording and the same personal and family requests. Even ministers often offer prayers before their congregations — sometimes at great length — which say nothing, expect no results and are not really intended to be answered.

Jesus scorned such elaborate, mindless prayers. "They think that they shall be heard for their much speaking" (Matt. 6:7). On the other hand, Jesus commended the short but earnest prayer of the publican, "God be merciful to me a sinner" (Luke 18:13). There are times when long periods of prayer are essential. Jesus prayed all through the night before times of crisis. There are times when we too should wait long upon God. Not only prayer, but reading the Scriptures, fasting and praising God with songs can all be useful at times like this. It is important to allow God an opportunity to speak to us so that prayer is not merely a one-way conversation.

Neither the length nor the posture of prayer is of paramount importance. Rather, as the law of successful praying states: *The primary elements of prayer are praying in Jesus' name, earnestness, faith and praying according to God's will.*

Manipulating God

How can I get God to answer my prayers? How we all want to ask this question! But it reflects a wrong attitude if by this we mean, How can I talk Him into doing what I want?

Surprisingly, God is more eager to answer us than we are to ask. He has told us to pray always and not to faint. He has made stupendous promises of the good things He would do for us if we would pray. To answer our prayers is His intention, or else He never would have invited us to pray.

At the same time, His intention is not to yield to every petition that escapes our lips. What a terrible thing if all prayers were actually answered! It would make God our servant if He always jumped at our bidding. We are instead *His* servants. Prayer is our means of communication with Him to learn His divine pleasure; to express our love and confidence in Him; to secure His guidance so that His perfect will may be done; to open our weakness to His strength and power. Virtuous prayer seeks to submit so that God can use us for His purposes — which are always, incidentally, for our welfare too.

God is not merely a force to be harnessed or turned on and off as we please. He is a Person with personal preferences we come to know as His will. His power is given to do His perfect will, not to be used as we please. The problem of prayer is not, therefore, to get God to answer, but to clear the way so that His answer can come freely. The answer has already been granted. It is already on the way while we are yet speaking. Only we can stop it from arriving!

But while God is willing to answer prayer according to His will, He has set up some ground rules which we must follow, for our own sakes and the sake of His kingdom.

The Golden Keys to Prayer

Would you like to revolutionize your prayer life? To remake it from a rusty tool, seldom used, into a ring of bright and golden keys that will unlock the doors of heaven and pour into your life all the glorious treasure God has for you?

The first and best key is vastly more important than most of us realize: *Praying in the name of Jesus*. God owes me nothing. I deserve nothing from Him except punishment for sins. Therefore all my earnest crying will not prevail unless I offer prayer in Jesus' name. Yet how many prayers have you offered implicitly in some other name? When God lets any such prayers come before Him at all, it is only because He knows we have to have *some* help, lest we perish utterly.

The name of Jesus is not a mechanical password. Tacking

"in Jesus' name" onto a prayer will not guarantee a favorable answer. Instead it should come from a deeply felt sense of our own unworthiness and Christ's worthiness. God will answer a prayer for Jesus' sake, even though He will not answer it for our sake.

Christ has power with God, which He offers to us. But we must declare our dependence on Christ's merits and disavow our own merits. A person who has learned this secret has also learned to trust in the Savior instead of his own unworthy works. All the angels in heaven hasten to attend to the prayer that is offered in Jesus' name.

Mean What You Say

How many prayers we offer with no real expectation of an answer! Some of us would be frightened if our prayers were taken seriously by God. Therefore *earnestness is the second key to successful praying.*

Pious-sounding prayers that tell God what He already knows, that use empty words or repetitions, are not taken seriously by us. We should not be surprised when God ignores them also.

It's been said that when we pray for rain, we should get our umbrellas ready! When we pray for God's power, we should get ourselves ready to act. When we pray for loved ones outside of Christ, we should expect them to come to Christ. When we pray for deliverance from an ungodly situation, we should pack our bags.

Prayer is more than mere wishing. It is getting down to business with God in such matters as health, finances, usefulness, safety, guidance, relationships and the kingdom of God. Some of the really striking answers to prayer in my experience have come only after such extreme exertion of will, emotion and mind that a life-or-death earnestness set in. "I will not let thee go, except thou bless me," said Jacob to the angel (Gen. 32:26), despite wrestling all night and getting crippled. His earnest prayer was answered.

Jesus in Gethsemane prayed in such agony the bloody sweat stood out upon His face. Elijah "prayed earnestly" (James 5:17) that it might not rain, and the sky withheld water for three and a half years. Thousands of Christians know what is meant by prayer warfare. The natural enemies of prayer — sloth, lust, Satan and selfishness — are always sniping at us during times of prayer. Only earnestness can propel a prayer far enough to break through the enemy fire and be heard by God.

Faith-backed Prayer

Faith is confidence in God's character and His intentions for us. Having faith as we pray assists us in stepping forward in boldness and determination.

Faith is certainly more than a synonym for a system of beliefs, such as the Baptist "faith" or the Catholic "faith." It requires little faith to accept doctrines and less to accept creeds. We may even believe these truths, yet have no real faith.

Romans 10:10 describes true faith as believing in the heart. Real faith, therefore, is a combination of intellect, feeling, will and surrender. With the mind we *believe*. With the emotions we *trust*. With willpower we *act*. As we surrender to God, we *submit* to doing His will.

Praying in faith must incorporate these elements. Skimping on even one will undermine effective prayer. For example, some people may believe in God but not trust Him. Their prayers are not answered. Some believe and trust but do not act. Yet faith without action, or works, is dead (James 2:17). Conversely, action without belief is futile and aimless; many good deeds are done by people who despise God. And the underlying attitude must always be one of supreme commitment to God, and that His will, not ours, will be the answer to our prayer.

How then do you secure faith? You cannot — it secures you. Faith takes possession of you as you meditate upon the love of Christ, the unshakable character of God and the good news of the gospel. "Faith cometh by hearing, and hearing by the word of God" (Rom. 10:17).

Faith blossoms only when we are assured that God really wants to demonstrate His redemptive love to us. A sense of security and courage comes into your heart when you lean on God with a certainty that He will not let you down.

God always begins to answer as soon as we begin to pray. His prophetic word is that "before they call, I will answer; and while they are yet speaking, I will hear" (Is. 65:24). But while the answer is definitely on the way — provided, of course, the conditions of acceptable prayer are met — it may take some time to arrive. This puzzles impatient Christians who are tempted to fear their prayers are not being answered.

There may be good reasons for God to take His time. Perhaps some lesson needs to be learned before we are delivered. Immediate answers might rob us of the benefit of valuable teaching through some experience. Perhaps our faith needs testing so it will learn to be strong and have power to endure. Perhaps there are sins which need rooting out or bad habits which need time to be outgrown. If the answer came too soon, we might never realize that certain things are offensive to God and thus need to be dealt with.

Hence, we are commanded, "Pray without ceasing" (1 Thess. 5:17). That is, pray persistently. Jesus told the story of a woman who kept pestering a judge until she got her request simply by wearing him out. God is not like the unjust judge of the parable, in that we must wheedle the answers out of Him. But if we sometimes get our requests out of the unjust by persistence, shouldn't we be even more persistent with the just Judge?

Don't Waste Your Time

No amount of persistence, however, will get God to act contrary to His will. Some prayers God simply cannot answer. Check your petitions alongside these failures:

"God, make me holy — but not yet." Saint Augustine prayed this prayer, but God refused to hear it. He relentlessly pursued Augustine for complete righteousness. We cannot buy God off by installments, nor appease Him by gestures.

"God, forgive me for what I am about to do." So wrote a movie actress upon her suicide. Yet this request poses a contradiction. How can God forgive without repentance first? Awareness of the need for repentance as we proceed into sin does not constitute repentance.

"God, let me do it — just once — then never again." The notion we can obey tomorrow while God winks at our sin today is a myth. What this prayer really asks for is a bargain with God — if He will forgo punishment on this immediate sin, we will then reform. God cannot entertain this prayer, because obedience is not a negotiable item.

"Lord, I thank thee that I am not as other men" (Luke 18:11). The "thanks" aspect of this statement is merely a coverup for blatant bragging. Is our goodness based upon comparison with others or with the demands of God? Our best righteousness is very faulty indeed, for God insists that all have sinned. Fancied superiority based upon religious orthodoxy is just as hollow as that based on education, race or social standing.

"Give me the Holy Spirit that I also may have this power" (Acts 8:19). When Simon the sorcerer said this, what he really meant was, Let me have that power so that people may be impressed with me. Ah, but God will not give His power for the gratification of man's ego. Peter responded that God could not grant the request because Simon's heart was not right.

Not My Will

Our inability to manipulate God to violate His will shows us the primary secret of effective prayer: "And this is the confidence that we have in him, that, if we ask any thing *according* to his will, he heareth us" (1 John 5:14, italics mine).

Jesus, who knew God's mind better than we do, left us an example of what John was talking about. Jesus prayed at Gethsemane, "Father, if thou be willing, remove this cup from me: nevertheless not my will, but thine, be done" (Luke 22:42).

Praying according to the will of God means asking for things which are His will to give us. God cannot work against His purposes. Our problem is to arrange our prayers so they seek His will instead of ours. "For we know not what we should pray for as we ought: but the Spirit itself...maketh intercession for the saints according to the will of God" (Rom. 8:26-27).

This is why we must call upon the Holy Spirit to teach us the mind of God. We should be guided by the Holy Spirit in the wording of prayers. His is the still, small voice that can be heard only if we quiet our own clamoring voice of desire and then listen.

The Bible contains the mind and will of God, laid forth in examples, principles and positive pronouncements. Many things are stated plainly to be His will. For these we need not question, but pray in absolute confidence. For example, "If any of you lack wisdom, let him ask of God...and it shall be given him. But let him ask in faith, nothing wavering" (James 1:5-6a).

However, not all situations are that simple. For these we must search the Scriptures to find where the wisdom of God is laid out in principle and example. Then we must submit to the quiet guidance of the Holy Spirit so that God's will may be known.

Spirit-led prayer becomes mighty. The number of answers will greatly increase because God is pleased to answer prayer according to His will. However, there are some common hindrances to prayer, as we will see next, that must be dealt with to have an effective prayer life.

TWELVE

DEMOLISHING PRAYER'S ROADBLOCKS

The law of unanswered prayer

One of the silliest lines I ever heard in a popular song says,

"I believe someone in the great somewhere
    Hears every prayer."

Such claptrap! The Father of our Lord Jesus Christ is not a mere "someone" in the "great somewhere." The Bible is perfectly plain as to where God is, what He is like and what He requires of those who seek answers to prayer. But, more to the point, the Bible says there are many prayers that get no higher than the ceiling of the room where they are offered. "Ye ask, and receive not, because ye ask amiss, that ye may consume it upon your lusts" (James 4:3).

> Behold, the Lord's hand is not shortened, that it cannot save...but...your sins have hid his face from you, that he will not hear (Is. 59:1-2).

Because prayer arises from our deepest emotional needs, it is often distorted by sentimentality, as evidenced in those song lyrics. Our task is to add to sentiment the light of truth and reason. This brings us to the law of unanswered prayer: *Unless we deal stringently with hindrances to prayer, we shall be puzzled as to why our prayers are not answered.* This chapter will look at some of the common obstacles to prayer: sin, doubt, selfishness, idolatry, stinginess, unforgiveness, love of money, cruelty, pride and covetousness.

Sin and Doubt

Of the many barriers to prayer mentioned in the Bible, the foremost is sin. How can we expect God to answer prayers when sin remains in us, thereby approving our rebellion against Him? Yet we should never become mired in guilt, making ourselves faithless and prayerless by an oversensitive conscience, because there is a simple remedy: Ask God for forgiveness. Then we can pray with a clean conscience.

A more difficult roadblock to overcome is unbelief. James 1:6-7 warns, "But let him ask in faith, nothing wavering. For he that wavereth is like a wave of the sea driven with the wind and tossed. For let not that man think that he shall receive any thing of the Lord."

Listen to the next prayer you hear — or which you offer. Is it spoken with a deep desire for a specific answer? Does real faith underlie it? Or does it merely address respectable words to God?

How do we remove unbelief and replace it with faith? Faith is a conviction about the character, love and integrity of God that produces trust in Him and results in bold, courageous action. Faith is not an emotion. You cannot get faith — real faith — by whipping your emotions into a state of excitement.

Faith is that unshakable confidence that caused Job to cry out, "The Lord gave, and the Lord hath taken away; blessed be the name of the Lord" (Job 1:21). Faith caused Elisha to command the waters of the Jordan to roll back by saying, "Where is the Lord God of Elijah?" (2 Kin. 2:14).

Faith is what Shadrach, Meshach and Abed-nego had in the fiery furnace: "God...is able to deliver us from the burning fiery furnace.... But if not, be it known unto thee, O king, that we will not serve thy gods, nor worship the golden image which thou hast set up" (Dan. 3:17-18).

Faith does not always demand understanding. It proclaims trust even when the mind is baffled. It is the soul's supreme defiance of the world, the flesh, the devil. It is not foolish soft-headedness, but it conquers by exultant and unshakable commitment to the unchanging God who demonstrated His love on Calvary.

Selfishness and Idolatry

"Seek ye first the kingdom of God, and his righteousness; and all these things shall be added unto you" (Matt. 6:33). We are familiar with this command of Jesus, but many Christians have rephrased it: "Seek ye first your own desires, and let God worry about His kingdom."

The secret of prevailing prayer is to be a lover of the kingdom of God and to seek its welfare constantly. Then much prayer for things becomes unnecessary because they come to us naturally as God willingly pours out His benefits upon those set on advancing His kingdom.

Selfish motives hinder prayer. "Ye ask, and receive not, because ye ask amiss, that ye may consume it upon your lusts" (James 4:3). Prayer that caters to pride, to love of things, to the protection of the ego, will not be answered.

A wife may pray for the salvation of a drunken husband so her home may be peaceful. That is seeking a good thing — for the wrong reason. We should seek the salvation of loved ones because they were made for God and have repelled Him. They are dishonoring Christ and ruining their souls. This is a proper motive for prayer — that God's kingdom may spread to include another rebel, for God's glory and that person's own spiritual welfare. Any side benefits to us are secondary.

Many people pray for the power of God, or the filling of the Holy Spirit, that their own egos may be bolstered with a sense of power. God is eager to give us power. But it is always given for service to Him and His kingdom.

The Holy Spirit comes not to excite us but to improve our disposition and use us more effectively in His service. If we seek the Holy Spirit merely to have a thrill or visible proof that God has come upon us — so we can have a "feeling" to talk about or to enhance our perceived spirituality — we may have an experience, but it will be more nearly akin to auto-suggestion. The test of a genuine experience of the Holy Spirit is whether or not our bad habits and tempers change and whether the kingdom of God is strengthened by our Spirit-filled service.

A strange verse tells us why God sometimes will not hear our prayers: "Son of man, these men have set up their idols in their heart...should I be enquired of at all by them?" (Ezek. 14:3). Idols in the heart, just like idols made of stone or wood, violate God's commandment to worship Him alone, for He is jealous. God is not jealous in the way we think of jealousy — envious, proud, spiteful. Rather He is tenderly solicitous of our welfare, refusing us the right to worship anything less than Him.

We cannot love our children too much. And the more dearly we love Christ, the more dearly we love our children, who belong to Him. Yet we put our children in the wrong place if we put them before Him, or their interests before His interests. To do so makes an idol of our children.

Many a man makes an idol of his reputation, business, possessions or hobbies. When these things, good in themselves, are put ahead of God, He cannot hear our prayers. There is one question that must be decided if we would have power in prayer: Is God absolutely first?

God often calls our attention to our idols by *not* answering our prayers. This can lead us to inquire of God, discover the idol and put it away. Then God hears our prayers.

A Heart of Liberality

One of the great hindrances to prayer is *stinginess*, the lack of liberality toward the poor and God's work. It is the one who gives generously to others who receives generously from God. "Give, and it shall be given unto you" (Luke 6:38).

For this reason, governments that promote ever-larger tax-funded welfare programs are at odds with God's kingdom because they diminish the role of Christian charity. By plundering from those who work hard, who practice the virtue of thrift and who would like to share their wealth as God leads, such governments make idols of themselves. They assume the God-like role of benefactor to all, the ultimate source of charity.

Yet charity is a virtue precisely because it is the result of free choice. Truly it is more blessed to give than to receive. It enables the giver, while providing an example of Christ's charity to us all.

One of the great prayer promises is, "And whatsoever we ask, we receive of him, because we keep his commandments, and do those things that are pleasing in his sight" (1 John 3:22). The context of this verse concerns giving to the poor. We are told to love, not in word only, but in deed. When we open our hearts to our brothers in need, we can have great confidence toward God in prayer. If we refuse, we can expect the opposite: "Whoso stoppeth his ears at the cry of the poor, he also shall cry himself, but shall not be heard" (Prov. 21:13).

The greatest promise in the New Testament regarding God's supplying our needs was given to a church that had invested gifts in God's servant Paul. "But my God shall supply all your need according to his riches in glory by Christ Jesus" (Phil. 4:19). Remember, this promise was given only to a certain group who qualified by first sharing with a needy minister who was imprisoned far away in Rome for the cause of Christ.

If you are seeking the reason for powerlessness in prayer, consider the vice of stinginess. Upon it many prayers have been hung up for years! God loves the generous heart.

The Release of Forgiveness

Have you forgiven *all* who have done evil to you? The Bible is uncompromising on this point: "And when ye stand praying, *forgive*, if ye have ought against any: that your Father also which is in heaven may forgive you your trespasses" (Mark 11:25, italics mine).

An unforgiving spirit is one of the most common hindrances to prayer. One reason God will answer prayer from sinners is that He has forgiven our sins. But God cannot deal with us on the basis of forgiveness while we harbor hatred toward those who have wronged us.

Are you wondering why some earnest prayer of yours is not answered? You may be among those paying a bitter price for the miserable gratification of nursing a grudge.

This is dramatically illustrated in the relationship of husbands and wives: "Likewise, ye husbands, dwell with them according to knowledge, giving honour unto the wife, as unto the weaker vessel, and as being heirs together of the grace of life; that your prayers be not hindered" (1 Pet. 3:7).

Spouses often forget that courtesy of speech is a Christian virtue. Instead they stir up resentment by shrewish displays of temper and speech. They nurse hostilities until they become hostile persons. Hostility arises only because they have not forgiven each other from the heart. It is not enough to forgive with words. Forgiveness must come from the very innermost being, the heart, or prayer will go unanswered.

Robbing God

We need not remain in doubt as to why some disasters come upon us. One of the great reasons for unanswered prayer — specifically the prayer for deliverance — is found in Malachi 3:8-11 (italics mine):

> Will a man rob God? Yet ye have robbed me. But ye say, Wherein have we robbed thee? In tithes and offerings. Ye are cursed with a curse: for ye have robbed me, even this whole nation. Bring ye all the tithes into the storehouse, that there may be meat in mine house, and prove me now herewith, saith the Lord of hosts, if I will not open you the windows of heaven, and pour you out a blessing, that there shall not be room enough to receive it. *And I will rebuke the devourer for your sakes, and he shall not destroy the fruits of your ground;* neither shall your vine cast her fruit before the time in the field, saith the Lord of hosts.

One measure of Christian maturity is whether money possesses you or you possess it as a steward of God. The love of money is the root of evil. The practice of tithing is a great step forward in getting on praying ground. It is God's way of setting us free from the tyranny of money. We return to Him a set portion of what He has allowed us to earn through the skills, time and strength He has given us.

Don't look for excuses, such as the notion that tithing is an Old Testament command not repeated under the new covenant. The New Testament assumes continuation of tithing. Hebrews 7:8 says, "Here men that die receive tithes; but there he receiveth them, of whom it is witnessed that he liveth." This was written around 64 A.D., well into the Christian era.

The Key of Kindness

God is kind. Further, Galatians 5:22 declares the fruits of the indwelling Holy Spirit to be gentleness, goodness, meekness and other kindred virtues. Yet Christians are sometimes unkind, thoughtless, malicious, hard-hearted, implacable, gossipy and even cruel. There is a "tiger" in every human heart. Even in a Christian, he sometimes breaks loose from his chains!

I shall never forget the shock of seeing a deacon on a fishing trip scrape the scales off a fish while it was still alive. Cruelty to animals is still cruelty! Cruelty to humans is worse. Cruelty to other races, the ignorant, the handicapped, the aged, the young, is an abomination to God.

Yet often our cruelty to people is more refined, and therefore more subtle and self-deceptive, such as words whispered behind someone's back. Have you cast all cruelty out of your life? If not, you will pray in vain.

Cruel words can damage other people and limit their usefulness. Cruel words can discourage new Christians so they do not grow. Cruel gossip sets one up as a judge in spite of the fact that God warns us not to judge others.

True Christianity is redemptive — it makes whole. It does not inflict wounds but binds them up. It restores and builds; it does not destroy and cripple. "The merciful man doeth good to his own soul: but he that is cruel troubleth his own flesh" (Prov. 11:17). The cruel man's troubles include erecting a hedge between himself and God that his prayers will not overcome.

Power Through Meekness

Pride was corrosive enough to change Lucifer to Satan. However socially acceptable pride may be, it is the Christian's worst enemy and the foe of answered prayer.

Pride is the love of one's supposed self. The true valuation of self cherishes what God can someday make of us to His glory, but pride feeds the inordinate love of the distorted image we have of ourselves. Out of this evil all others arise.

We perceive ourselves to be clever and become proud. We boast of our accomplishments, which in perspective are rather shabby at best. Isaiah 64:6 likens our very best attempts at being good to being clothed with filthy rags. A look at the real self is frightening but wholesome.

The Pharisee, proud of his religious achievements, went to the temple to pray and bragged. The publican beat on his breast and asked for mercy. Jesus said God would not hear the proud Pharisee, but absolved the humble publican.

There is nothing more offensive to God than prideful prayer. We have nothing of which to boast. All is of grace. We deserve nothing but judgment. The wonder is that God can find anything in us worth loving.

"God resisteth the proud, and giveth grace to the humble. Humble yourselves therefore under the mighty hand of God, that he may exalt you in due time" (1 Pet. 5:5-6). God will exalt the meek through His answers to their prayers.

Whatever talents we have are gifts on loan from God and should be used in trust. When we take credit for our talents, we are fools, for God can take them back in a flash. A heart that refuses to steal credit from God is a yielded heart. God answers the prayer of humility because it comes from one set on doing God's will — one who is convinced that no

117

fleshly attributes will enable him to meet that calling.

Misplaced Love

Many Christians indulge in idolatry without ever realizing it. The vice involved is subtle but real: covetousness. Ephesians 5:5 says it is an idol.

Covetousness is the desire to acquire what God does not want us to have. We usually think of coveting material things, but covetousness is not limited to possessions.

One of the greatest trouble-roots Christians have is the "will to power." It may be manifested as the will to dominate others, or the will always to be right, or the will to monopolize conversations. Whatever its form, it still exalts self and lessens dependency on God. It puts a clear barrier between our prayers and God.

This is not to say that all ambition is sinful. Ambition for the self-fulfillment of God's gifts and callings is wholesome. But ambition for the sake of the ego is not only evil, but can never be satisfied. If it ever does reach the heights of power and possession it has coveted, it weeps because there are no more worlds to conquer.

Yielding to wrong desires can make us pray for harmful, even sinful, things. Before we can learn to pray, we must surrender our desires to Christ and want what He wants.

We must deal sternly with self's voracious appetite and cry, "Be silent, you foolish and selfish desire!" We must develop the virtue of contentment. Only then can we learn the joy of an inner poise that is not dependent upon things. And then we will have eliminated a major hindrance to prayer as we sharpen our spiritual focus on what God wants, not what we want.

Once you have demolished your prayer handicaps, you can confidently expect to see progress in your spiritual walk. Read on, and you will see that God has many purposes in prayer that exceed the mere granting of requests.

THIRTEEN

HONING YOUR PRAYER SKILLS

The law of prayer's purpose

Mark Twain described it as an unexpected prayer meeting. As a trolley car neared the top of Pike's Peak, its cable slipped. Suddenly prayers and promises were uttered out loud, their fervor increasing as the runaway car hurtled down the mountain. Desperate passengers made vows. Tears of repentance flowed.

Then the car came to a stop. Most riders, realizing their safety, began to joke about their "undue nervousness."

So much prayer is like this — instinctive, even sincere, but none too impressive with God. This chapter will examine how common types of prayer — for healing, financial aid, emergencies, guidance, overcoming bad habits and intercession — can be more effective than the Pike's Peak plea bargains.

There are some distinctions about these prayer categories, but they are all similar in this respect: To be effective, they must be in accord with the two prayer laws already presented. That is, we must first deal with hindrances to prayer, and our prayers must be based on earnestness, faith, God's will and the name of Jesus. If those conditions are met, we may well see the answers to prayer that we expect.

However, there is something more fruitful than going for a high prayer batting average. It is stated in the law of prayer's purpose: *Prayer's highest goal is not to fill our requests but to harmonize ourselves with God's eternal purposes.*

Prayer for Healing

As all Christians have experienced, God is not our butler-doctor. He does not answer every healing-related prayer as we would like Him to. But, as we will see, He has His reasons for allowing sickness and death and for providing different means of healing.

God created our bodies with remarkable, miraculous self-healing powers. Of course, there are times when the body cannot naturally do, alone and unaided, what is God's intention for us. Then we must use medicine, therapy or specialist physicians. Drawing upon medicine and doctors is no sin — God has provided them to serve us.

There is much sickness due to sin. We release the flow of the destructive influences within our spirit when we behave contrary to God's will, and this eventually affects our minds and bodies. Healing in such instances has a direct spiritual remedy: repentance.

Other healings of the body go beyond medicine, doctors and hospitals. With terminal illnesses and permanent handicaps, there is nowhere else to turn for healing but to God. Also, there may be instances where we have faith that it is God's will to heal us of routine problems more expediently than through traditional methods so that He can glorify Himself to the world through a healing that is clearly miraculous.

Is healing provided by the suffering and death of Christ? Certainly. But there is more to it than merely having a correct view of the atonement. Christ died to demonstrate God's willingness to forgive sins and also God's willingness to bear our sicknesses with us. Yet we cannot conclude that this automatically ensures us of perfect health. To do so would ignore that God deals with us individually.

There are times when only through sickness can we be brought into the fullness of God's perfect will. Sickness is sometimes a rebuke for sin. Sometimes it becomes a warning. Occasionally it is used as a refiner to rid us of dross. It can be a means through which the Holy Spirit drives us to depend on Him.

Even Jesus did not escape suffering. "Though he were a Son, yet learned he obedience by the things which he suffered" (Heb. 5:8). This mystifying passage says that the body of the divine Son of God was not delivered from all pain in order that God's purposes could be wrought.

This is not to say that sickness is God's will. Rather, sickness is going to come, and God can use it for His glory if we will turn it over to Him.

Steps to Divine Healing

The first step in securing God's power to heal our ills is to cast out those things that hinder this healing. We cannot expect Him to heal us of alcoholism if we keep drinking, for example.

Next, in our prayer for deliverance, we must want what God wants. Few Christians doubt that God *can* heal. God healed in Old Testament times. Jesus healed. The disciples healed. Paul healed. Down through Christian history, instances of healing apart from human means have been documented reliably.

But the big question is: Will God heal *you*? The answer is that, in most instances, *He is healing you now!* Since it is usually His will to heal you, mighty spiritual forces already are hard at work for your healing. Part of the problem is to remove things that block God's healing power. Just as we've seen certain things can block any effective prayer, similar things can stand in the way of a miraculous healing: greediness, overindulgence, negative thoughts, a foul disposition, immoral relationships, secret vices, inordinate ambitions, hatred, an unforgiving heart, a hostile spirit or rebellion.

You will pray in vain for healing until you deal with these hindrances, asking the cleansing of Christ and the indwelling of the Holy Spirit. Then you will be ready to replace these negative attitudes with confidence, faith and obedience. It is not enough to get rid of the bad. Unless it is replaced by the good, a spiritual vacuum is left, and the bad eventually comes back in — much worse than before.

Let your mind dwell on such thoughts as: God loves me! God wants to use me! God can use me best if I am yielded to Him! I want God's will! I will vow to serve Him as never before whether I am healed or not!

Next, go to the Bible and see all the places where God has shown His power to heal. This will prepare your faith, for "faith cometh...by the word of God" (Rom. 10:17). The father of a demon-possessed boy asked Jesus "if thou canst do anything." But Jesus put the burden back on him, "If thou canst believe, all things are possible" (Mark 9:22-23). The "if" belongs to us, not to God.

If you are prepared to pray in faith, believing God's healing response is on the way, then pray with all your might. This, of course, is no formula for sure-fire success. Remember that Paul had some kind of affliction for which he sought relief (2 Cor. 12). Three times he sought God to remove the thorn in the flesh. God gave him strength to bear it instead of removing it. God informed Paul the affliction must remain, so as to keep him keenly aware of the present world after his astounding visions of heaven, which might have made Paul lose hold of earthly reality.

But do not let this experience weaken your faith. The whole teaching of the Scriptures is that the times when God withholds healing are exceptions rather than the rule! If He does delay or withhold healing, it is because He has some higher good in mind. God can heal *all* kinds of diseases, though He does not heal in every single case — or else we would never see a Christian die.

In that light we need to realize that for the Christian death is not altogether a tragedy. In many instances it is the good gift of God. It is the natural conclusion of physical life. It must neither be courted nor feared. God and Christ stand behind the curtain, and to go to them is joy, not terror.

Praying for Financial Aid

Do you ever face bills you cannot pay? Do not delay talking it over with God until His assistance becomes a last resort. God is an ever-present help in time of trouble, but He can do more for you if you seek His counsel first in all business matters.

Not only is God concerned about our daily bread, He is concerned about how we earn it. The Bible teaches that He gives us strength to earn money. But we cannot ignore the principles of thrift, saving and frugality. God has not promised to deliver the wasteful. Nor has God promised to bless the lazy, the foolish spender or the status-seeker.

For financial deliverance we must pray to God for things to work out *for His glory*. Our motives must be pure. We must deal with problems such as the failure to tithe or the failure to put God's kingdom first.

When in financial trouble, make vows of obedience to God. Remove unnecessary drains upon your income. Read the promises of God concerning deliverance and prosperity. Ask God to honor your faith and obedience. Place your trust in His loving care.

Be sure what you seek is reasonable and consistent with God's will. Hold on in faith to God's love, and do not lose hope.

If these conditions have been met, help is on the way — perhaps from an unexpected source. Financial trouble may come to drive us to our knees in prayer, so go there and cling to God's promises till the answer comes. Take solace in David's words, "I have been young, and now am old; yet have I not seen the righteous forsaken, nor his seed begging bread" (Ps. 37:25).

Prayer in Emergencies

It was common to hear in World War II that there were no atheists in foxholes. Under the terror of battle, many men instinctively turn to the God they had ignored when no emergency was present.

Does God respond to such prayers? Generally, yes. David wrote, "This poor man cried, and the Lord heard him, and saved him out of all his troubles" (Ps. 34:6).

While God may hear such prayer, do not presume it is by any means the most effective way to approach Him. We will all face emergencies. Those who best cope with them, however, are those who are prepared spiritually. Here are four key points:

• A habit of daily prayer helps you meet the unexpected with poise and confidence. You will already be prepared, and your prayer account will be paid up — ready to draw on when needed.

• Praying in emergencies is effective when there is no continued state of rebellion. What a tragedy to call upon

God and find so many barriers built up through sin that we cannot get through to Him! Some emergencies occur to shock people into repentance. This is valuable, but only if it lasts.

• Emergency praying will be much more effective if we are already disciplined by the principles governing prayer.

• We should fill our minds with the positive promises of God and then, when emergencies arise, act with confidence and assurance. God's response to prayer is largely up to us.

Prayer for Guidance

The voices of those who readily pray for a financial quick fix, for healing and for many other things often are strangely mute when it comes to asking for guidance. God, who sees the end from the beginning, and who plans for us to fulfill ourselves by doing His purpose, will guide us — but only if we ask.

Our tendency is to go it alone. Like Milton's Lucifer, we would rather rule in hell than serve in heaven. The Adam in us still lusts for forbidden fruit. In the midst of a confusing situation we prefer to thrash about, when all the time we could find the certain path if we would but look up toward God.

Sometimes our greatest need in the quest for guidance is to feel our need of it, since we usually want not guidance but God's approval of our own plans. Anyone who actually wants God's guidance may have it. But God wants to control, not merely advise.

How odd that we flee from the embrace of divine love! Do we think God will mislead us or mistreat us? Hardly, for Romans 8:28 promises that God causes all things to "work together for good to them that love God." Then why do we flee from His will?

Because we rightly suspect that to be enfolded in His embrace may require a loss of self-sufficiency. God has given us a self — or, more properly, made us a self. The self is spiritually restless until it finds its rest in Him. Yet we resist this rest because we cannot trust divine love.

Prayer is often a struggle to the death between self-will and divine will. When we surrender, prayer for guidance rises swiftly to the throne, and the answer is on the way! God's clock always strikes on time. The answer of guidance will come unless we set back the hands.

Praying About Bad Habits

Habit is a momentum which keeps us going in a certain pattern or direction without conscious decision. Bad habits differ from good habits in that there is more compulsion in those that are bad.

Most wrong habits, such as alcoholism, are compounded by a sickness of the will. Paul wrote, "For the good that I would I do not: but the evil which I would not, that I do" (Rom. 7:19). Paul says the only solution to this dilemma is *God*. There are two main steps to take in overcoming bad habits:

• Find out why you have allowed them. Are they caused by environment, evil companions or an inner weakness? Take steps to change the environment or its power to enslave you. Face the necessity of dropping harmful friendships for the glory of God. Find the legitimate strength for inner weakness by discovering what hunger you have that is striving for fulfillment in the wrong way.

• Ask God to help you find His resources for the evil that has gripped you. You may not be able to ignore the hunger — the craving for cigarettes, the desire to watch sensual movies — but you can change the way you appease it.

Beware of mere naked reformation. This may have momentary virtue, but there is a more excellent way. Too many overcome a bad habit only to exchange it for pride or for something else just as bad. As you pray to cast out the unclean spirit in the name of Christ, fill the vacuum with a good habit, or else you will fall easy prey to the bad habit again in a moment of weakness.

Evil habits must not be cut down but cut out. There is no compromise, because little roots will grow back rapidly. Surrender the evil to Jesus, and ask Him to fill you with Himself and with service to His kingdom. Stay away from temptation. Stay close to godly people. Pray for hourly strength.

Prayer for Others

Abraham prayed for Sodom, Moses prayed for Israel, Samuel prayed for Saul and Jesus prayed for His disciples. Jesus interceded for you too, praying in the upper room "for them also which shall believe on me" (John 17:20) through the disciples' word.

Likewise, all believers are commanded to pray for others. Intercessory prayer keeps our petitions from being too self-preoccupied. They lift our sights from immediate problems and cause us to look at the whole kingdom of God. God wants us to work, so He drives us to prayer first and then out to work in the harvest field.

One of the greatest functions of prayer is to intercede for the salvation of others. Not that we need to convince a reluctant God to save them. He is eager to do that. But for reasons known best to Him, we are required to pray for the Holy Spirit to convict them of their need of God.

Experience has proven that when much prayer is offered for a particular person, he or she usually comes to Christ. Perhaps we touch an invisible current of power which God reserves for those who pray the prayer of intercession. People for whom prayer has been offered in faith for many years have been known to come to Christ even after the death of the one who interceded.

There is no need to pray for the dead. But we should pray

for the salvation, healing, deliverance, prosperity and spiritual growth of those we know. Our prayer list should grow and our compassion with it. As a side benefit, we will find it difficult to criticize those for whom we pray.

Prayer and the Bible

One of the simplest ways to improve prayer accuracy is to stick to the Bible. As you grow in prayer experience, you'll find that prayer apart from a biblical foundation is like shooting a shotgun without looking down the sight — you spew out lots of words, you have little idea where they're going and you probably will miss the target. Biblical prayer is like a well-aimed rifle shot — a single projectile that goes exactly where it's supposed to go.

Prayer without the accompanying use of the Bible suffers from lack of direction, assurance and power. He who would master the practice of successful prayer must master Scripture. The Bible is God speaking to us — a necessary prerequisite to our speaking with God.

Genesis contains the prayers of Abraham and Jacob. Deuteronomy gives much space to the prayers of Moses. At least one-third of the Psalms are effective model prayers. Solomon, Daniel and Nehemiah prayed powerfully. The Gospels, notably John 17, record the prayers of Jesus. The New Testament closes with a written prayer. These are model prayers because the ones praying them submitted themselves to God, and they obtained answers.

Furthermore, the Bible contains prayer promises covering almost every human need. George Müller, one of the greatest prayer warriors of the last generation, would find a specific promise before he prayed. With his finger on the text, he would then claim the promise of God. Over five million dollars for his orphanage in England came in answer to prayer.

As we can see from close examination of these many areas

of prayer, there is more going on than simply filing our requests with a heavenly commissary. While God may answer prayer immediately in the way we imagined, at other times He uses our prayers to work out His will in every area of our lives. This may be through His silence, His delay in answering prayer, His pointing out certain displeasing things in our lives, or His provision of an unexpected answer to our prayer.

In other words, the larger meaning of prayer is to harmonize oneself with God's will. Through the combination of Bible and prayer we are able to grow in our total knowledge of God's overall purposes. We are better able to cope with life's ordinary problems that, as the next chapter will show, are also part of God's plan to mature us.

FOURTEEN

PRECIOUS PROBLEMS

The law of the source of our troubles

Does trouble in your life seem like a wasp sting? Suddenly trouble pricks the little bubble of our routine life. We resent it and fight back, hoping to deal with it quickly and ruthlessly. We are tempted to think trouble is that which interrupts a normal life, a complacent existence. In actuality, though, we know better. Every person experiences trouble. In fact, many people are in trouble more than they are out of it. Job 5:7 confirms this observation: "Yet man is born unto trouble, as the sparks fly upward." Trouble is a guest who has worn out his welcome.

As surely as sparks head upward, our lives are constantly drifting through troubles.

This leads to a somewhat startling conclusion: *God apparently considers trouble necessary.* If He didn't, He wouldn't have placed us in a world filled with trouble. Man is born to breathe, love, eat and, among other things, face trouble.

This becomes a little easier to accept when we consider its parallel in natural physical laws. When we exercise, we introduce trouble in the form of resistance. It may be the lifting of weights or the overcoming of our body's inertia to run from here to there. Yet our muscles are strengthened through the process of conquering that resistance.

Automobile travel consists of overcoming gravity, which tries to hold us in one spot, and friction, which constantly slows us down. Yet travel changes us — from one environment to another. By overcoming resistance we grow, we become strong. In a broader sense, God has designed a life of trouble for us so that we will grow mentally, physically and spiritually.

Acceptance of trouble is basic to mental health. One reason people commit suicide is their refusal to accept man's destiny of trouble. One reason for crime is that men take matters into their own hands after failing to deal with routine trouble, such as lack of money or interpersonal problems.

Consequently, there is a law of the source of trouble: *Unless we understand God's purposes for trouble, we will not mature.*

Sources of Trouble

There are three primary sources of our troubles. First is the *limitation of time.* In the gaze of eternity, our lifespans are but a blink. We have only a little time to get an education, build a career, support institutions, amass enough wealth to get through our lifetime and, throughout all this, to do whatever God has called us to do.

Job 14:1 confirms that soon after we are born, we begin the lifelong struggle against time: "Man that is born of a woman is of few days, and full of trouble."

We get into many of our troubles because we're in a hurry. And why the rush? Because we know we have but a short time to live.

A second source of trouble is the *poison of pride*:

> Hear ye, and give ear; be not proud: for the Lord hath spoken. Give glory to the Lord your God, before he cause darkness, and before your feet stumble upon the dark mountains, and, while ye look for light, he turn it into the shadow of death, and make it gross darkness. But if ye will not hear it, my soul shall weep in secret places for your pride; and mine eye shall weep sore, and run down with tears, because the Lord's flock is carried away captive (Jer. 13:15-17).

Be not proud, because pride brings darkness. Distress will come. Give glory to God before your feet stumble upon the dark mountains. Pride is the father of all sins and therefore the source of many of our troubles.

Why do people murder? The world is too small for two certain people to coexist, so one shoots the other. It's pride at its destructive worst. Much of our trouble is due to an unwillingness to let others triumph. We must override them, put them down, resent them when they slight us, get back at them when they degrade us, because no one else must be permitted to rise higher than we are.

Why did Adam and Eve eat the forbidden fruit? They desired knowledge that God had told them they shouldn't have. They were too proud to do without it.

But Jesus taught us to have the opposite attitude as we relate to others. If someone takes your coat, give him your vest. If somebody compels you to go a mile, go two miles. Christians need not worry that their rejection of pride will mean a life drowning in trouble — an unceasing stream of giving away possessions and extra-mile service that exhausts you beyond recovery — because we have One who will lift us above earthly troubles in His perfect timing: "Humble yourselves therefore under the mighty hand of God, that he may exalt you in due time" (1 Pet. 5:6).

The third source of trouble is *misuse of the natural desires of life*. The primary ones are money, sex and power — all good in themselves, but subject to extreme abuse.

It's normal to make money. When we receive a paycheck, that money is simply our work, time and talent in a negotiable form. Then we trade it to somebody else for the product of their thought, time and talent.

Sex is one of God's greatest pleasures given to men and women. Not only does it add depth to the marriage covenant, but it is essential to the continuation of life on earth.

Power is everywhere. It's manifested in governments, churches, armies, families and individuals.

In a world that still operates under the curse of Adam, money, sex and power are subject to the pull of sin. Hardly a day goes by that headlines do not reveal burglaries or embezzlements, respected leaders caught up in a sex scandal or politicians abusing their privileges through self-serving initiatives. It's been said that 90 percent of our trouble in life originates in the misuse of money, sex and power.

Gaining From Trouble

Just because we face limited time, just because our human natures are poisoned by pride, just because we are constantly tempted to misuse the natural desires of life does not mean these elements have to be nothing but stumbling blocks. What can we do to use our trouble best?

We can learn from trouble. The psalmist records in Psalm

119:67, "Before I was afflicted I went astray: but now have I kept thy word." When we do wrong, we get into trouble. But in that trouble we learn to follow God better and to keep His Word. We will learn from our problems if we have a heart to do so.

We can turn to God as our refuge. "The Lord also will be a refuge for the oppressed, a refuge in times of trouble" (Ps. 9:9).

Are you suffering today? God intends that the trouble should drive you to Him. Not only is God a refuge, He is an active assistant to us. "God is our refuge and strength, a very present help in trouble" (Ps. 46:1). We can get alone with God to find peace of mind, to search our hearts, to receive guidance or help.

Yet we tend to turn to God only after trying every other way out of our trouble. Finally we say, "Well, I guess I'm going to have to pray," as if this is the *least* effective remedy. God should be the first One to whom we turn.

There are times when we simply need comfort. Have you ever seen how a mother comforts a hurt child? Sometimes it matters not whether the mother can solve the problem, but just that she will listen as the child shares his anguish.

Paul recognized God as the source of comfort: "Who comforteth us in all our tribulation, that we may be able to comfort them which are in any trouble, by the comfort wherewith we ourselves are comforted of God" (2 Cor. 1:4). Isn't that a beautiful verse? God, in comforting us, can help us comfort others. He has suffered. He suffers with us. He puts the arm of consolation around our shoulders.

Why Me, God?

Finally, in learning to get the most of trouble, *we should seek God's purpose in trouble.* Hebrews 12:9-10 highlights the aspect of discipline that God brings about through difficulties: "Furthermore we have had fathers of our flesh which corrected us, and we gave them reverence: shall we not much rather be in subjection unto the Father of spirits, and live? For they verily for a few days chastened us after their own pleasure; but he for our profit."

Fathers may lash out at their children in angry frustration, because fathers are not always right in the way they handle a troublesome child. But God, our Father in heaven, is always right. He allows trouble to enter our lives to chasten us for our profit:

> Now no chastening for the present seemeth to be joyous, but grievous: nevertheless afterward it yieldeth the peaceable fruit of righteousness unto them which are exercised thereby. Wherefore lift up the hands which hang down, and the feeble knees; and make straight paths for your feet, lest that which is lame be turned out of the way; but let it rather be healed. Follow peace with all men, and holiness, without which no man shall see the Lord: looking diligently lest any man fail of the grace of God; lest any root of bitterness springing up trouble you, and thereby many be defiled" (Heb. 12:11-15).

People are sometimes bitter because they have failed to appropriate the grace of God. Their troubles, instead of profiting them, making them more holy and peaceable and causing them to grow, have created bitterness. God prefers that we respond to the trouble He allows by receiving His grace — that is, His free forgiveness and mercy. By accepting His Son as our Savior and the fullness of His death on the cross, we can allow God to work out His purposes in us.

We will see next that many troubles are spiritual. Unlike certain physical circumstances that we can do little or nothing about, God has remedies for us to deal with spiritual problems.

FIFTEEN

DIGGING
FOR ROOTS

The law of the treatment
of spiritual problems

As a baby, Achilles was dipped into the waters that would make him impervious to the stroke of the sword or the point of an arrow. However, according to this legend, his submersion covered every place except where his heel was held. So when Achilles came to the great fight, at first nothing could harm any part of his body. But finally an arrow pierced his heel and caused his death.

Centuries after this Greek myth, we still refer to someone's "Achilles' heel." This means an unprotected or weak spot. Each of us has at least one spiritual Achilles' heel — a set of spiritual difficulties tailor-made to our personality, our own weaknesses, our strengths. Satan, of course, has great interest in striking at our weakest point. He is not an adversary to be taken lightly.

An evangelist once advertised, "I am out to battle Satan." I hope he had the shield of the Lord with him. As my father, who was a preacher, advised me: "Don't ever try to battle Satan in your own strength. He has been in business for six thousand years, so he knows more than you will ever know."

How right my father was! Because Satan is so clever, beyond our wildest imaginings and best defenses, we must adhere to the law of the treatment of spiritual problems: *We must not allow spiritual problems to linger or try to fight them in our own strength, but we must go to God and His Word for the power to cut them out at the root.*

Our Vulnerable Strengths

While Satan enjoys targeting our weaknesses, he is also crafty enough to attack us at our strongest place, or somewhere in between. The danger is in supposing our strong places are so well-entrenched they do not need much guarding. That's where Satan may be able to prance right in.

The same war in which Achilles fought illustrates this point. The gates of Troy were so strong it would be difficult for a Greek raiding party to survive the arrows and the molten lead that would be poured down upon them had they tried to attack. So the soldiers of Greece created a wooden horse of such amazing proportions that when the people inside the city saw it, they were eaten up with curiosity.

The Greek fleet sailed away, so the Trojans went out to the plain to inspect the strange wooden horse. Still intrigued, they dragged it into the city, not knowing that inside was a small contingency of Greek soldiers.

During the night, the Greek fleet came back to shore. The soldiers inside the horse crept out and opened the gates that could not have been battered down from the outside. The Greek army sacked the city.

Years ago I stood amid the ruins of Troy, and that fabulous story came to mind. I thought how the city fell at its strongest place because of the weakness of the people.

The Diagnosis of Sin

Because Satan is so quick to exploit our spiritual weaknesses, as well as the fleshly strong points that through self-deception we may leave unprotected, it is imperative that we root out all spiritual problems.

The first thing one must do with spiritual problems is face their manifestation, just as the first step in dealing with physical ills is to acknowledge that we have symptoms that do not agree with health.

If you are like me, you tend to follow this pattern with physical problems: You suffer a pain or a sense of unease. Whether that unease is disease you don't know. So you take two aspirins, go about your business and, if the pain disappears, you forget about it. But if the pain is twice as bad the next morning, you really worry. Another day goes by, and you start complaining to your family or anybody else who will listen. Maybe by the fourth day you decide you'd better do something about it, so you go to the doctor.

Spiritual problems are like physical problems — you don't solve them until you face them. Perhaps you have often been overcome by a certain behavioral mistake. As a first step, you must become aware that the infection of sin is spreading and that you are incapable of curing it.

Next, examine yourself. That means look realistically at yourself without alibis. When you can explain away what is wrong, you will not take action. As long as you can say a physical problem is merely indigestion, you will put aside the possibility that it might be a heart attack building up. With spiritual problems Satan is quick to stir the imagination with excuses — that the problem is not really worth dealing with; that the problem will work itself out with time; that no one is perfect, so even Christians should expect to live with a fault or two.

Self-examination is scriptural: "Examine yourselves, whether ye be in the faith; prove your own selves. Know ye not your own selves, how that Jesus Christ is in you, except ye be reprobates?" (2 Cor. 13:5).

Customized Sin

When you have determined what the problem is, you may not even know from where it arose. Why should you have a problem of lust or avarice (the desire to acquire)? That leads to the next step — *going to the textbook*.

Many physicians know from experience what illness a person suffers from merely by examining him. On occasion, though, a doctor must go to a medical library to learn what a particular set of symptoms may indicate. Christians also have a textbook, a casebook and an authoritative source of diagnosis: the Bible. In it you will find the different kinds of spiritual problems laid out, explained so that you can understand them.

There are some sins that do not tempt me in the least. There are some that do. The same is true about you. There are sins that fit what psychologists call your personality profile. Those are your "besetting sins," based on the Hebrews 12:1 reference to "the sin which doth so easily beset us."

You can walk through a field of tall grass with wool trousers on and emerge with all kinds of cockleburs stuck to your clothing. That is the way besetting sins are. As you walk through life, they grab hold of you, even though you don't want them. The Bible can help us pinpoint the root of our problems by helping us identify what kind of besetting sin we have.

Actions of Sin

There are seven basic classes of sin.

There are sins against God. You can live a very good life in the community and in your family, but inwardly you may sin against God. As King David confessed, "Against thee, thee only, have I sinned" (Ps. 51:4).

You can sin against yourself. For example, "He that committeth fornication sinneth against his own body" (1 Cor. 6:18).

We can sin against others. This is so common that Jesus included it in the Lord's prayer: Forgive us our sins, as we forgive those who have *sinned against us.*

We can sin against society. First Peter 2:13-14 says Christians are to submit themselves to civil authorities. To do otherwise brings disgrace to the name of Christ.

You can sin against the light. Did you ever stop to think that your own energy is insignificant compared to that of the sun, yet you can shut the sun out just by closing your eyes? The light of God constantly shines upon our problems, but if we shut our eyes or turn a deaf ear, it is sin. Yet this is human nature, as we saw with the law of man's natural tendency, which is flight from God. "Men loved darkness rather than light, because their deeds were evil" (John 3:19).

You can sin against the truth. Bearing false witness, distorting, lying, telling things out of context, making our opponents look worse than they are, not living the truth — all these are sins against the truth.

Finally, we can sin against Christianity itself. Hebrews 10:28 recalls how, under Mosaic law, serious transgression received the death penalty. So then, "of how much sorer punishment, suppose ye, shall he be thought worthy, who hath trodden under foot the Son of God, and hath counted the blood of the covenant, wherewith he was sanctified, an unholy thing, and hath done despite unto the Spirit of grace?" (Heb. 10:29).

If you do something contrary to what you know Christianity stands for, it is a grave sin. If we sin against Christianity, which has shed so much more light than the Law of Moses, we have even fewer excuses than Old Testament sinners. The Bible says we deserve a stricter judgment.

Conditions of Sin

These seven classes of sin are actions. There are three others that are conditions of sin. A *state* of sin is usually worse than an *act* of sin. Consequently, our spiritual problems are more likely to arise from a state of rebellion against God than from a single act of rebellion.

Three states are reprehensible in the sight of God. They are contagious, spreading spiritual disease in the soul of man. These states of sin, characteristic of those unsaved, can come back in and infect a Christian if he is not careful.

Blindness. Jesus spoke often about spiritual blindness, and He was not talking about ignorance. Perhaps a person cannot help ignorance; spiritual blindness is intentional. As Samuel replied to King Saul, who had selfishly refrained from killing much of the Amalekite livestock and the Amalekite king, "To obey is better than sacrifice, and to hearken than the fat of rams. For rebellion is as the sin of witchcraft, and stubbornness is as iniquity and idolatry" (1 Sam. 15:22-23). Saul, trying to justify his failure to obey Samuel's prophetic word, thought he could close his eyes to God's will and get away with it. He couldn't.

Stubbornness. Determination is a virtue. Stubbornness is a vice. When God speaks to your conscience and you say, I won't, you are showing your stubbornness. This could be the root of your spiritual problem. God's greatest charge against the people of ancient Israel was that they were a stubborn and stiff-necked people. And we are their spiritual descendants!

Pride is the third of this trinity of wretchedness. Pride puts *self* on the throne and ousts Jesus from kingship. It opens the door for every kind of sin.

How to Be Cured

David's Psalm 139:23-24 provides a divinely inspired prayer: "Search me, O God, and know my heart: try me, and know my thoughts: And see if there be any wicked way in me, and lead me in the way everlasting." If you will pray that prayer in honesty, God will come past the roadblocks of your prejudices and reveal your problem. There are four ways in which He points you to the problem:

• Whatever you most frequently try to avoid thinking about is very close to what is wrong with you. If you don't mind discussing all kinds of sins, but find yourself saying, "I don't want to talk about that" when a certain area comes up, then you've got a good clue.

• Where we are consciously in opposition to the Word of God by our beliefs, behavior or relationships, there lies the root of a problem.

• When you do something about which you are prone to rationalize, and your conscience bothers you and you try to silence it, you are near the real problem. When you sense that God is not going to answer your prayers because that problem — that sin — keeps coming into your thoughts, that may well be a road sign pointing to your real problem.

• Beware when you reject the warning or pleading of sincere Christians or counselors. We have counseling ministries in the church because we cannot always see our problems clearly, and we need to talk them out with someone who understands. If we cling to our own way despite the entreaty of Christians who have no ax to grind but are speaking about God's will from an objective point of view, we know we have come quite near our problem.

143

Don't run. Don't hide. Don't be like the prophet Jonah and go in the opposite direction from God's directive and hope it will be all right. Jonah probably rationalized, "I can set up a prophet's ministry in Tarshish." Yet until Jonah faced up to his disobedience of God's command to go to Nineveh, he couldn't get enough victory over his spiritual problem to set up ministry anywhere.

One of the hardest things about the diagnosis and treatment of spiritual problems is to make a decision. The key is in the timing, and the right time is always *now*.

The prodigal son, having squandered his wealth, was reduced to feeding the hogs. He got so lonely he probably even talked to them after a while.

"You fat hog, I have to eat what you are eating," he might have said. "I am a Jew, and we Jews don't touch hogs. I am so hungry I have to eat the husks that I feed you! Even a servant in my father's house is better off than I am."

The son was wallowing like the pigs, except his pen was filled with the mud of self-pity. Then, in a startling turnabout, he rose above the mire of worldly life that his own rebellion had driven him to: "I will arise and go to my father, and will say unto him, Father, I have sinned against heaven, and before thee, and am no more worthy to be called thy son: make me as one of thy hired servants" (Luke 15:18-19). He wanted to get out of that hog pen. *He made a decision to do so.*

Whatever your spiritual problem is today, hear the word of the Lord. Say to yourself, I will arise and go to my Father. It is the decision to go *now* that counts. God will be faithful to help you with your problems.

The sooner we deal with spiritual problems, and the more careful we are to cut them out at the root, the more attuned we will be to hear God's voice and fulfill His will. This is no small advantage. As the next chapter will show, it is not always easy to pick out God's voice from the many voices competing for our attention.

SIXTEEN

SORTING OUT
THE VOICES

The law of
influences

As Christians, we try to make decisions according to Scripture. Some of us may even believe that God's written Word is the only influence on our choices. But we kid ourselves if we don't recognize that there are other voices clamoring for our attention. Each one desires to be dominant and make us obey. Vance Packard, who wrote *The Status Seekers* and other popularizations of sociology and psychology, concluded that people are directed in one of three ways: by tradition, by others or from within.

But there are two other voices he did not mention — the

voice of Satan and that of God. So there are five voices at work on each of us.

Except for the satanic influence, there is something good to say about all other kinds of direction. They are not always wrong. The problems arise more on the matter of emphasis or balance.

Hence the law of influences: *We can never have success until we accept Christ and discern the different voices of the world, Satan and God.*

The Voice of Tradition

A Democrat speaking at a political rally punctuated his remarks by asking the crowd to vote for him.

Every time he did, an ornery old lady would say, "I'm a Republican!"

He would ignore her and talk further about why they should vote for him, and she would interject, "I'm a Republican!" He finally became so exasperated that he asked, "Lady, just why are you a Republican?"

"Well, because my father was a Republican."

"Why was he a Republican?"

"Well, because his father was a Republican."

"All right, lady. If your grandfather had been a donkey, and your father had been a donkey, what would you be?"

She replied, "I'd be a Democrat."

That lady was directed by tradition. The voice of tradition so overwhelmed her in this area that she may have been deaf to current truth.

Perhaps somebody told you back in 1953 that the Dodge was a good car, so you've been buying Dodges ever since. The truth is, some years they are better than others, like most everything else. Yet tradition, providing a simplistic answer to the complex problem of evaluating the best car for your needs, may well misguide you.

Jesus had more trouble with tradition-directed folks than

any others. He rebuked them for substituting traditions for the commandments of God (Matt. 15:3).

This does not mean tradition is of no value. I wouldn't want to be without traditions in terms of my appreciation of America. I truly believe in our great national heritage and the traditions that go with it. The Old Testament is full of God's commands for His people to establish traditions and maintain them so His legacy would continue. The danger is that we can let tradition become the dominant voice speaking to our hearts.

The Voice of Others

One of the saddest verses in the Bible is 2 Timothy 4:10: "For Demas hath forsaken me," Paul wrote from prison, "having loved this present world."

Demas for a while was outwardly Christian, but apparently he never belonged to Christ in his heart. He evidently didn't love Christ with all his might. He may have been reared in a godly environment. He was certainly the product of a church, but deep down he loved this present world. So when the going got tough, he forsook the work of God and clung to the things of the visible world.

Demas was directed by others. Other-directed people don't have a mind of their own; they prefer whatever is popular.

A particular car may be the best-selling model in the nation. Fine, but it doesn't necessarily mean that particular make of car fits your needs. Maybe the manufacturer merely has the best advertising.

When you begin listening to the voice of popular trends telling you "everybody's doing it," beware. After all, this is the same seductive voice that leads so many young people into trouble.

Whose voice we choose to listen to determines our allegiance. "Friendship of the world is enmity with God"

(James 4:4). We cannot cozy up to the pressures to conform to the world's ways without alienating God.

The Voice of Self

Ayn Rand was an atheist whose books exalted individualism. She also believed strongly in capitalism, yet her compelling self-interest led her to reject altruism — willing devotion or giving for charitable causes — that often flows from individuals and companies prospering in a free-market society. The true spirit of altruism has its roots in Christianity. We Christians wouldn't get very far with God if the good Shepherd had not made the ultimate altruistic act, laying down His life for the sheep. When a person is self-directed only, all things are judged only by himself. He serves God, if he serves Him at all, on his own terms. He takes his cue for life's decisions from the lyric popularized by Frank Sinatra, "I did it my way."

Perhaps the worst poem ever written is Ernest Henley's *Invictus*. He chants, "I thank whatever gods may be for my unconquerable soul. I am the master of my fate, I am the captain of my soul."

Many people are drifting through life, steered by Captain Self. They may think they are the masters of their fate, but they too will one day come before the throne of God, who will determine their next port of call. Every knee shall bow before the Lord Jesus Christ. The question is, will it be now while it does some good? Or will it be when we are forced to our knees by the mighty hand of God, when it is too late?

The challenge is to serve God on His terms, not ours, dictated by the voice of self. For example, Sunday is the Lord's day — all day. That means the day is *His*, not ours. We are to do those things on the Lord's day which are pleasing to Him, not consider it a day when we can do whatever pleases the self and its whims.

Some people won't even consider tithing, and many of

them claim to live by the Bible. But how do they reconcile their attitude with Malachi 3:8-9? "Will a man rob God? Yet ye have robbed me. But ye say, Wherein have we robbed thee? In tithes and offerings. Ye are cursed with a curse: for ye have robbed me, even this whole nation."

God's standard for giving is tithing, and more. If you really belong to Him, if everything you have belongs to Him, it's no burden to tithe, because it is His money to start with. You are just giving it back to Him.

Young person, where are you going to college?

"Well," you reply, "I haven't decided yet."

What you ought to say is, "The Lord hasn't yet guided me in this matter." Does it ever occur to you to take God into consideration for decisions such as this? Your mind belongs to Him. He doesn't want it filled with ideological garbage. He has a perfect will for every decision, including where you are educated.

I once prayed for a young person who blew his brilliant mind on drugs. Now this young man can't get back in focus, and unless Jesus Christ gives him a miracle of healing, the great promise of his early life will never be fulfilled. He was determined he would go his own way. He was self-directed. If more young people could see such cases firsthand, they would know God is concerned about their place of education. It was in college that this young man became involved with drugs.

It's in these everyday decisions that we find out whether we are inner-directed or God-directed. "All we like sheep have gone astray; we have turned every one to his own way" (Is. 53:6). Those who are directed too much by self are in for a rough, unpredictable trip.

The Voice of Satan

"Let no man say when he is tempted, I am tempted of God: for God cannot be tempted with evil, neither tempteth he any man" (James 1:13). We cannot blame our sin on God's voice or some imagined testing from God. "But every man is tempted, when he is drawn away of his own lust, and enticed. Then when lust hath conceived, it bringeth forth sin: and sin, when it is finished, bringeth forth death" (James 1:14-15).

When we yield to temptation and are led astray, it comes from our lusts. But that's not the end of the story. "But I fear, lest by any means, as the serpent beguiled Eve through his subtlety, so your minds should be corrupted from the simplicity that is in Christ" (2 Cor. 11:3).

The serpent — the devil — beguiled Eve. He played upon her lusts. Lusts cause our downfall, but Satan is the one who plays his tune on that sensitive harp in our souls. Ephesians 6:11 advises, "Put on the whole armour of God, that ye may be able to stand against the wiles of the devil." "Wiles" means trickery or craftiness.

Those captured by Satan's deceit, who fail to don adequate spiritual armor, therefore, are demonically directed. This is not to say Christians will never hear the voice of Satan, for we will. But God's charge to us is to discern Satan's voice, refuse to obey it and seek God's voice instead. We do this with the help of our Ephesians 6 armor: girding our loins with God's truth, putting on the breastplate of righteousness, shodding our feet with the gospel, holding up the shield of faith, putting on the helmet of salvation and wielding the sword of the Spirit, the Word of God.

The Voice of God

A lot of people think that only a church-abiding Christian with calloused knees hears the voice of God. Hardly so! *Everybody hears from God.* But that doesn't mean everybody recognizes His voice; or if they do, that they obey it; or that what He says is always comforting.

Romans 1:19 says, "Because that which may be known of

God is manifest in them; for God hath shewed it unto them." God can be known by every human being because He makes Himself manifest. All you need to do is look at the creation, and you can understand the Creator.

Yet the following chapter of Romans shows that God reveals His kingdom in even more explicit ways: "For when the Gentiles, which have not the law, do by nature the things contained in the law, these, having not the law, are a law unto themselves: which shew the work of the law written in their hearts, their conscience also bearing witness, and their thoughts the mean while accusing or else excusing one another" (Rom. 2:14-15).

We can be certain God speaks to all people and that they are accountable, because His law is written on everybody's heart, Christians and non-Christians alike. Since God speaks through the conscience, it becomes the vehicle of God's voice in the soul. That's good up to a point, but we need the written Word of God as well as the voice of the conscience.

There are, then, five main voices: tradition, others, self, Satan and God.

The Father speaks in every man's heart. The Judge of the universe has branded His law on the consciences of men. We know it instinctively because we are spiritual beings. When the voice of God speaks to the conscience by the Holy Spirit, it's about His holiness, His creativity, the purpose of life, His existence and our sin. We hear this voice whether we want to or not.

Hearing on All Five Cylinders

Do you really want a full, well-rounded Christian life? One where you are in the middle of God's will and gaining favor in the eyes of man as well as God?

Then pay your respects to tradition, but don't be tradition-directed. Pay your respects to others, but don't be other-directed. Pay your respects to self-reliance in business and other things, but don't be self-directed.

Learn to recognize the voice of Satan so you can tune him out. By all means be God-directed, but understand that if you want God to direct your life instead of merely judge your life, you'll have to receive His Son. If you've already received Him, guard yourself from slipping out from under His control. Jesus will gladly speak to you, but repeated disobedience will dull the sound of His voice. Yield your life to the voice of Christ, and you will experience the kind of success every Christian dreams of: "If ye abide in me, and my words abide in you, ye shall ask what ye will, and it shall be done unto you" (John 15:7).

SEVENTEEN

LIFE'S BALANCING ACT

The law of triads

The word "triad" is well-known to musicians, but it is not commonly used among most people. It simply means a group of three, as in a musical chord of three notes.

The concept of three comes from mathematics — and if we look closely, we can see mathematics at work in every phase of life. For example, a musical scale consists of a progression of notes whose tones can be expressed mathematically. Using math, we can predict the combinations of those tones that produce harmony, as well as those that produce discord.

In chemistry, mathematics helps predict which chemicals can bond to form molecules and how strong those bonds are. One cannot be a chemist without being a skilled mathematician.

What might be called the laws of nature are actually mathematical laws. The laws of gravity, magnetism, the expansion of gases, precipitation — all such laws can be expressed mathematically.

Just as God has created order in the physical universe, He has created order in the spiritual world. One foundational component of His order is that many principles of the physical and spiritual realms are manifested in groups of three. Hence, we have the law of triads: *God's perfect balance for life is revealed in three-part unities.*

Blessed Trinity

Until Jesus Christ came, there was no clear revelation of the holy trinity or the personhood of the Holy Spirit. The Holy Spirit is mentioned in the Old Testament more or less as a synonym for God. No clear delineation is made between the Father and the Holy Spirit, and only in prophecy is the Son of God prefigured. The Old Testament contains implications of a multi-personed God, but the trinity was not understood by the Jews of that day.

It was not until the baptism of Jesus, where the Holy Spirit came upon Him and the voice from heaven said, "This is my beloved Son: hear him" (Mark 9:7), that man had the full revelation of God as a holy trinity: three persons, one substance. One God, three manifestations.

The earliest intimation of the trinity is in Genesis 1:26: "And God said, Let us make man in our image." "Us" and "our" are plurals, implying the doctrine of the trinity. It remained for the apostle John to elaborate: "In the beginning was the Word [his favorite name for Christ], and the Word

154

was with God, and the Word was God. The same was in the beginning with God. All things were made by him" (John 1:1-3).

In other words, God the Father, God the Son and God the Holy Spirit — the divine trinity or triad — were present and all working at the creation. It was this trio that said, "Let us make man in our image."

Omnipresent Triads

Since we are created in the image of a triune God, we should be able to find many evidences of the trinity in our lives, our minds, our behavior and our relationships.

For instance, man is composed of body, soul and spirit. The soul corresponds to God the Father; the body to Jesus Christ, who was incarnate (put in a body); and the spirit of man to the Holy Spirit. Every person is body, soul and spirit, reflecting God, who is Father, Son and Holy Spirit.

Happiness is composed of three major ingredients. One is *love* — both the act of being loved and the ability and opportunity to love. Take love out, and we can never find happiness.

Second, *fulfillment*. We all have talents and abilities, but if we don't get a chance to fulfill them, we're never going to be happy.

Third, *significance*. We've got to be somebody. How often have we heard someone protest, "He didn't treat me as if I was anybody, but as if I were a thing to be used and disposed of." Conversely, someone might say, "He really treated me as if I was *somebody*." Significance is the foundation of all ambition — that inner drive to count for something, to achieve, to prove we as individuals have worth and being.

Take out one of these ingredients — love, fulfillment and significance — and the balance that makes up happiness falls apart.

We cannot balance a stool with two legs. We can balance it with four or five or ten, but three legs are absolutely essential. And so it is with man. Unless he is balanced in the various triads, so that there is equal weight on each of the three legs, he will fail. The path to a successful Christian walk is to understand the triads of life. They form the scales by which we can tell whether or not we are in balance.

Second Peter 1:9 explains, "But he that lacketh these things [faith, virtue, knowledge, temperance, patience, godliness, kindness, love] is blind, and cannot see afar off, and hath forgotten that he was purged from his old sins."

Then Peter says: "Wherefore the rather, brethren, give diligence to make your calling and election sure: for if ye do these things, ye shall never fall: For so an entrance shall be ministered unto you abundantly into the everlasting kingdom of our Lord and Saviour Jesus Christ" (2 Pet. 1:10-11).

What is the price attached to maintaining a balance in faith, virtue and so forth? Peter implies that those who ignore this balance are going to slink into heaven rather ashamed of themselves because they busied themselves with selfish pursuits. But they will make it to heaven because they trusted in the grace of Christ.

Others who embraced the balances associated with godly character qualities will find the heavenly streets thronged with people eager to make them feel at home. Peter calls that an abundant entrance, a hero's homecoming.

The Triad of Time

Notice the three time dimensions in 2 Peter 1:9. The *present* problem is blindness. "Cannot see afar off" relates to the *future*; "hath forgotten that he was purged" relates to the *past*. We cannot ignore the past, present or future and maintain a balanced walk with God.

Man's keen awareness of past and future is one quality that separates him from animals. An animal isn't even cognizant of the present as something distinct from the past and future. He simply exists and enjoys it.

But man is both cursed and blessed with amazing faculties that encompass all three perceptions: past, present and future. This triad of perception is one of the evidences that human beings are made in the image of God, who inhabits eternity. God knows everything that is past, is present, and that is coming in the future.

We fall short of God's omniscience, but we have obvious reflections of this broad perception: hindsight, foresight and insight. Hindsight helps us understand history and how we arrived at our present state. Foresight enables us to project into the future with prophetic understanding. Insight aids us in understanding the present and the underlying meaning of things.

Essential Triads

Mankind's selfhood, the ingredient that makes us who we are, is rooted in a triad: *intellect* (mind), *feeling* (emotions) and *will* (volition). Not surprisingly, these too are characteristics we share with God, in whose image we are made.

How do we know God is not a force like gravity or electricity? How do we know God is not merely a powerful and benevolent influence? We know He is a Person because that which makes a person is intellect, feeling and will, and we can find vivid examples in the Bible of His manifesting all three characteristics.

Though we've never seen God, never touched, tasted, felt or smelled Him, we know He exists. Why? Because we can discern traces of intellect, feeling and will in His creation. What makes us a person makes God a Person. What makes us a triad makes God a triad.

Another triad is illustrated by man's environment — *inner* (psychic), *outer* (social) and *upper* (spiritual).

We always have an inner environment despite our physical location. We can be in jail and yet create our own world by withdrawing into ourselves. Albert Einstein did this when he attended boring parties. He testified to withdrawing into his own mind to enjoy thinking great thoughts. We live our lives for the most part inside ourselves, a secure hideaway known only to us. Nobody can intrude there.

We also dwell in an outside environment: the world around us, people, family, friends, coworkers and the nation.

Third, we enjoy an upper environment. This is our spiritual life, where communion with the heavenly Father is found.

God has also established a basic threefold hierarchy of authority: *self, society* and *God*. Any political or philosophical worldview that denies this triad rebels against the God-given pattern. Communism, for example, demands from its people only the obligation to society. It denies responsibility to God and the right to look upon self as an authority. But Christianity espouses God first, others second and self last. We can order these areas in priorities, but we also must balance them.

The Balanced Life

Man should have a threefold balance in his life — among *worship, work* and *play*. Show me a man whose life is mostly work and no play and no worship, and I will show you a man so badly off balance he doesn't know what life is all about. But it is also possible for some men to be overbalanced on the side of worship. It is said that such people are so heavenly minded they are no earthly good.

Did you ever stop to think that play is a part of God's plan for your life? Play isn't something that God has no part in, though it too can grow too large in your life. In fact, one of the devil's main tools to destroy people spiritually is to convince them to substitute work or play in God's place of

158

preeminence.

The triad of balance also is seen in man's outlook on life, whether *optimistic, pessimistic* or *realistic*. The optimist maintains that the glass is half full. The pessimist contends it's half empty. The realist simply takes it as it is.

Realism might appear to be a safe perspective because it's middle ground, but there's danger in being overly realistic. The realist is sometimes blind to truly pessimistic circumstances. We kid ourselves if we think there isn't anything wrong with the world. And there are times to be acutely aware of those wrongs. When I consider how man has outraged the laws of God, I'm a pessimist. I'm a pessimist when it comes to believing that man can save himself. I'm a pessimist when it comes to believing the world is going to cure its own ills. It's not. But I'm an optimist when I look at Jesus. I'm an optimist when I see that God has a plan for my life, and He is willing and able to work it out.

But to be exclusively a pessimist or an optimist is wrong. Sometimes we need to be optimistic even though things look bleak. On other occasions we need to be pessimistic when things look bright. And there are times when realism would make us amble along on an ordinary pathway when we ought to be flying, bubbling with enthusiasm and excitement. So realism alone isn't sufficient either.

Pursuing Success

The prescription then for a successful life: *Understand that life is a series of many triads, and examine them to check for balances that will lead us to success, happiness and usefulness.* They are indeed the key to a fulfilled life.

But since all of us are off balance somewhere, we come to know wisdom, success, happiness and fulfillment gradually as we attempt to bring the triads of life into balance. That's why we have the church. That's why we have the Bible. That's why we have Christ. That's why we are made in the image of God.

How intricately God has constructed life! With what care has He fashioned us — not only as a body, but also as a soul and a spirit. He created all these laws so we could find personal joy, usefulness in society and service to God. As the final part of this book will show, God has great plans for us — if we but adhere to His kingdom laws — to find complete fulfillment in our earthly life. And He has even greater plans for us to reign with Him in heaven.

PART 3

OUR DESTINY IN CHRIST

EIGHTEEN

COURAGE
UNTO VICTORY

The law of
faith

The entire ministry of one of our age's great Christian leaders has been encapsulated by the phrase "the power of positive thinking." I read everything he puts out. I preached in his pulpit in New York; he preached in my pulpit in Texas. And he discovered something the church had long overlooked: It had become too negative. So when Norman Vincent Peale rediscovered the power of positive thinking, he did the Christian world a great favor.

His friend and fellow minister, Robert Schuller, has become known for an expansion of that truth: the power of possibility thinking. What a valuable contribution his ministry has made!

I would like to have my ministry — and yours — known for a principle that is akin to positive thinking and possibility thinking, yet slightly different. It is the succinct law of faith: *Faith is the victory*.

Not By Sight

Our minds cannot comprehend the breadth of victories God has in store for us if we but develop our faith muscles. And there is no more important truth for enhancing our victories over Satan and discouragement than 2 Corinthians 5:7: "For we walk by faith, not by sight." This crystallized truth is a guide for conquering our circumstances in the time of illness, disappointment, grief or loss.

Many people think faith is simply working on your imagination, pumping up your inner man until you are pepped up inside and out. That isn't faith at all. You may encounter times when your inner man needs encouragement; you may need to hear about the powers of possibility thinking. "For we walk by faith, not by sight."

"To walk" in the Bible means to live the daily Christian life. You first come to know Christ by faith, and you walk with Him by faith each day of your life. The walk of faith transforms us as we move along God's ordained path, continually finding ourselves in a new spiritual place.

You may not see yourself as a salesperson, but suppose you have a car you need to get rid of. Go about your task, and suddenly you are a salesman! If you look closely, we're always selling something. I sell the gospel of Jesus Christ, and, like Paul, I can honestly say I am not ashamed of it.

Paul said he was not ashamed of the Father's product because it carries the power of God unto salvation. Who is ever ashamed of power? I'm not, because the victorious Christian life is one of power. I want to sell you on the truth that God wants you to be an extraordinary person of extraordinary achievements brought about by God's extraordinary power. And the key to that truth: "We walk by faith, not by sight."

Anything that comes through the five senses — seeing, hearing, tasting, smelling or touching — is natural and good. But the gospel doesn't come through the five senses. Rather the gospel comes; God honors you; God opens new doors; God makes you a success; God rescues you from trouble; God brings meaning into your life — through faith.

Our challenge is to nail down faith. What is it? How do we get it? How do we use it?

Principles of Faith

Faith is more than belief. You may believe that America is the best country in the world. But if you're not working for America by defending it or helping to preserve our country's values, then you don't have any faith in it. You just have belief in it.

We face the same test in our relationship with God. You can believe there is a divine god. You may even believe in the true God. But don't expect mere belief to carry much weight with Him. James 2:19 cuts to the core: "Thou believest that there is one God; thou doest well: the devils also believe, and tremble."

In addition to belief, faith incorporates *trust, action in obedience* and *permanent commitment.*

Picture a bridge over a dangerous chasm. You think, I believe that bridge is safe. Are you across the chasm? No.

Then you think, I'm going to trust that bridge. I believe in the engineers who made it. I trust them and their handiwork. Are you across? No!

Only when you step onto that bridge and walk across the chasm can you find yourself on the other side. Belief, trust, action and commitment translate you from uncertainty to victory. That is what James meant when he said, "Faith without works is dead" (James 2:26). Or to paraphrase, "Faith that is only belief and does not result in trust, action and commitment isn't faith at all — it's only belief."

I want all of us to belong to churches of faith — not just churches which carry the danger of glorifying man's efforts, but churches of *faith*. Your church should be the house that God built in response to your faith, without giving any credit to man.

When I was about to become the minister of our church in Glendale, California, I was reluctant to accept the call. But God broke through beyond my senses. "You're not much of a servant," He said. "I'm not too proud of you, but I'm going to do a work through you. And if I do, it will be obvious that you didn't have much to do with it, that you were too flawed. All the glory will come to Me." I accepted that word on faith. I stepped across my own chasms of doubt — which all of us have — to find God's success in my life.

Opportunities for Faith

The truth of walking by faith and not by sight will transform you, because Jesus wants to walk with you every day. He has set before us difficulties and other circumstances to which we can apply our faith and see it grow.

Young man, young woman, you may be facing an exam at school. It may mean a lot to you. Go home and study so well, so thoroughly, that you can say, "Lord, I did my very best." Then, in faith, take that examination. You'll come through, for we walk by faith and not by sight.

Sunday school teacher, are you having a difficult time in your class? Before you blame your students, check yourself. Are you visiting your pupils' homes? Are you praying over each of your pupils as you prepare your lesson?

If you are not taking these steps of faith, you won't transform your students. You will be merely entertaining them or keeping them quiet for a while. But once you begin preparing to the best of your ability, with faith expecting God's power to move, you will see a difference in your class. Lives will be changed.

When I was fifteen, my father held an evangelistic meeting for a pastor in Spartanburg, South Carolina. This pastor built a rough, wooden "tabernacle" in which to hold his services. There was sawdust on the floor.

Yet in the midst of these humble surroundings, there on the platform was a new, shining Hammond organ! Now this was during the Depression, when Hammond organs were a new invention. Even the big churches could not afford them. It was the musical equivalent of a Rolls Royce.

"I just don't understand," my dad said to the pastor. "You were hardly able to buy enough wood to build this auditorium with the help of your men, and you've got sawdust on the floor. Yet you've got a brand new Hammond organ. How are you going to pay for it?"

The pastor replied, "I haven't paid for it. I went down to the dealer and told him the Lord wanted us to have it."

"The dealer answered back, 'Well, if the Lord wants you to have it, so do I,' and he put it out here on the platform. But he added, 'You're going to have to hear from the Lord in the next thirty days.' "

The preacher told my father, "I've got fifteen days to go and haven't gotten any money in yet."

Dad said, "That's foolishness. You should have had the money in hand and then bought the organ."

"Dr. McBirnie," the preacher said, "don't you believe God will honor my faith?"

That pastor had not acted foolishly. He did something in faith for the glory of God. God honored his faith by providing the money for that organ.

I pray God will make your church known for its mighty faith. Let the sick come in, be anointed with oil and prayed for. Not with the typical prayer for the sick that at best makes people feel a little better, but a prayer that believes God *heals* the sick.

Let those who are faced with financial problems come to our churches to pray or meditate. Let them hear that God supplies all their need according to His riches in glory in Christ Jesus (Phil. 4:19).

Let people go to others and say, "Pray with me; I'm in trouble. Pray with me; I'm discouraged."

Let people say of your church, "You just can't go inside that place without feeling a great spirit of faith."

Oh, that God would give us the gift of faith!

The Fifth Dimension of Faith

As I have fallen on my face before God, crying, "O Lord, make ours a church of faith," I have discovered another ingredient of faith. We must exercise belief, trust, action and steady commitment. But the fifth element is *courage*.

Unless faith results in courage and includes courage, it isn't really faith at all. Something is missing. The life goes out of it. Winston Churchill said courage is the virtue that makes all other virtues possible. How right he was!

If faith is to be the transforming principle by which you operate, glowing in your life like a light lit from within, then it will require courage. Moses held his rod over the Red Sea, and it parted. It took hours for the Israelites to pass through on dry land while God held the waters back. Moses had to possess courage to expect that kind of miracle and trust God to protect the lives of the entire Hebrew nation.

Jesus' promise that the gates of hell will not stand up against the church was not given to a church whose members would be content to sit in the bleachers. When the church batters on the gates of hell and takes the offensive in faith, those gates will fall. The church will not prevail just because it is the church; we need courage to undergird active faith.

A Call for Courage

A Baptist preacher told me how he was preaching in Czechoslovakia when a woman in her early twenties accepted Christ. She was the first to be counseled, but because she was laughing and seemed too giddy, she was dismissed, and others were counseled.

"But after we left about 11:30 that night, the young lady was still there," the preacher said. "She came back in, now very serious. She began asking questions such as, 'What happens if I sin tomorrow?' I talked with her for ten or fifteen minutes, and finally said, 'This is a difficult situation.'

"For at that time in Czechoslovakia, every citizen was being interrogated about their attitudes toward the Russian invasion of 1968. People had one of two choices. If they lied and said the Russian invasion was a great thing, they were let go. If they disagreed with the invasion and told the truth, their futures were wiped out."

This lady was to be interrogated the next morning. It would certainly be a lie for her to endorse the invasion, since her husband lay at home, paralyzed by a shot in the head from gunfire during the invasion. So she was really asking, "Can I now, as a Christian, lie to secure my future?"

The preacher told me, "I was about to share with her that promise of our Lord to those who would be brought before authorities: 'Take no thought what you will say; the Holy Spirit will give you words in that hour.' Suddenly God spoke to my own heart and seemed to say, 'You cannot claim this promise unless you are willing to do My perfect will.'

"So I shared with her the promise — and the conditions. Her head dropped, and for a long time she was almost in another world. Suddenly, with tear-filled eyes, she said, 'I will do the will of God at any cost.' "

How can a young woman who just met Christ make such a tremendous decision so quickly? The answer is that she saw the will of God for her life, recognized that was all that mattered and decided to do it. God honored her faith, and the authorities dismissed her case.

This woman learned in a hurry that courage is part of faith. Had she skipped that fifth element of faith, she would not have had this spirit-building experience of truly walking by faith. She was changed upon salvation, but God already had in store for her a greater maturity. You too will find that if you begin to walk by faith in each decision of your life, God will transform you. You will never again be the same.

Walk by faith, not by sight. Never depend upon your feelings, for they will change. All that really matters is what God says. What does His character indicate? What does His trust assure? When you believe God, act upon your faith with trust, commitment and courage.

NINETEEN

READY FOR RECKONING

The law of gifts and talents

A mechanic can fine-tune an engine to perfection while it is on a testing block. It may reach a level of harmony that results in a relatively quiet hum, giving little evidence of the violent explosions taking place many times per second inside the piston chambers. But not being harnessed in a car or truck, this dynamo of power simply spins. It goes nowhere. It contributes nothing.

We too can become like that engine. Commitment to Christ does not guarantee that our gifts — our internal combustion — will be harnessed to the external purposes of God for His creation.

We were created as unique individuals. Likewise, each of us has a unique contribution to make. Opportunity to make that contribution is one of the strongest ingredients in happiness.

Yet too often we waste or misuse the gift God has given us. To do so is to consume that gift for selfish purposes, to thwart the purpose of God for our lives. This leads to disillusionment, bitterness, unfulfillment and the shattering of dreams. The endless search for satisfaction that so many people experience today is often a direct consequence of misusing their gifts.

As we will see, we are all privy to gifts. Even people we might consider ungifted have not been ignored by our heavenly Father, who gives a wide variety of gifts, all good. Hence the law of gifts and talents: *God grants to everyone gifts in trust, and we must give an account for how we use them.*

Three Basic Gifts

There are three kinds of gifts that come from God. The first gifts are *those that we are given at birth as our biological heritage.*

I read of a twenty-three-year-old computer genius. He squeezed about $12 million worth of equipment from a telephone company by tapping into their computers and placing orders through the system.

Then he got caught. The judge sentenced him to forty days in prison, and the police made him a computer security consultant (an unusually sensible law-enforcement decision). Now this man has his own firm, helping companies to ensure their computer systems will not be used against them.

The line between the misuse of one's gifts and the proper use of them is very thin. Yet the consequences can be as broad as the difference between serving a jail sentence and owning your own successful business.

This computer buff didn't learn that much about computers at school. Nor did somebody take him aside to train him. He was born with that aptitude, or gift, and he developed it to its fullest extent, though without a moral foundation.

The second category of gifts is *spiritual, given freely by God to all those who seek them*. The Bible mentions two prominently — salvation and wisdom.

Most non-Christians think everybody will be saved, in the sense of going to heaven, especially if they've led "good" lives. They will be in for a big surprise unless they change.

The Bible says all men are lost, and only those who trust in God's provision for salvation, Jesus Christ, will be saved. This salvation is a gift. It is not earned by what might be called good living, and it does not get canceled by sin.

The Bible also speaks of wisdom as a gift. Most successful businesses do not depend on one smart person, but a pool of committed people whose shared smarts and experience enable the business to cope with problems and daily tasks. Likewise, we need to ask wisdom of God, who desires to be our partner in success.

He is a willing consultant: "If any of you lack wisdom, let him ask of God, that giveth to all men liberally, and upbraideth not; and it shall be given him" (James 1:5). Notice the word "any." This gift is not limited to pastors or the college-educated; it's available to anyone who will ask.

The third kind of gift is *a special talent that is bestowed by God for special service to man and God's kingdom*. It is to be used entirely for God's glory.

Where do we get the aptitudes that are a part of us at our physical birth? Partly from our parents' genes. These are the traits to which we refer when we say, "He was born with an artistic ability."

The same thing is true in the new birth. We are born again with certain gifts which God wants us to use for our fulfillment, the blessing of other people and the kingdom of God.

The Bible calls these spiritual gifts. First Corinthians 14:1 encourages us to "desire spiritual gifts."

Some spiritual gifts are given at the new birth. Some of them are given by a special recognition of the church, such as an ordination. For example, Paul wrote, "Neglect not the gift that is in thee, which was given thee by prophecy, with the laying on of the hands of the presbytery" (1 Tim. 4:14).

Other spiritual gifts are given by the moving of the Holy Spirit across the congregation and electing us. Some are given simply by one's being filled with the Holy Spirit.

Paul elaborates about spiritual gifts in 1 Corinthians 12: "Now there are diversities of gifts, but the same Spirit. And there are differences of administrations, but the same Lord. And there are diversities of operations, but it is the same God which worketh all in all. But the manifestation of the Spirit is given to every man to profit" (1 Cor. 12:4-7). The Spirit gives gifts of the word of wisdom, word of knowledge, faith, healing, miracles, discerning of spirits, tongues and interpretation of tongues.

Giving an Account

Whether gifts are conferred at birth, given freely to all who ask or bestowed by God for service to God and man, there is one thing in common: *We are not to take credit for them.* This is the first part of the law of gifts and talents: Gifts are given by God — not chosen by us, not earned — and hence are not to be objects of pride. They are to be exercised in trust.

The second part of the law is this: Because these talents are given in trust, *we must some day give an account for them.* "For unto whomsoever much is given, of him shall be much required" (Luke 12:48). The versatile person will be required to give account of his many gifts in the same manner as a less gifted person. "For we shall all stand before the judgment seat of Christ.... Every one of us shall give account of himself to God" (Rom. 14:10,12).

Christians shall stand before the family judgment seat of Christ, what Scripture calls the *bema*, and non-Christians shall stand before the great white throne of judgment (Heb. 9:27). This final judgment is the time of reckoning to justify God in His having treated each person with justice.

Non-Christians will be judged on their rejection of Christ. Because they have totally misused their talents, they shall be forever banished. But Christians who come before the *bema* shall be rewarded in precise proportion to the faithfulness with which they have used their talents. They will be judged for their *stewardship*, their faithfulness to oversee property and power in trust for somebody else.

God wants to give His people wealth so that we might have what we need, so that life might be abundant. But if we stop there we are no better than the non-Christian. God wants us to earn all the money we can in order to be a better steward for Him, for even the ability to earn money, which is the most common ability in the world, is of God.

Some preach that money is the root of all evil, but that's not true. It's the *love* of money (1 Tim. 6:10) that is so named. If we use money to be a better person and to be more useful to the kingdom of God, we will be given all that He can trust us with. What the Bible condemns is loving money, using it selfishly, using it destructively, and leaving it to people who haven't earned it and who are likely to misuse it.

In the area of wealth, there are signs that reveal where our hearts are really focused. One is how we draw up our wills. How we wish our life's accumulations to be used, when there are no more self-centered needs to be met, reflects how we view our stewardship over what God has given us.

Somebody writing a biography of the Duke of Wellington said the most revealing thing about him was his checkbook stubs. They showed what he cared about or didn't care about.

What if our checkbook was opened at the judgment of

God? Would we be ashamed? God has promised He will reward the steward who has been faithful over a few things by making him ruler over many.

The Requirement of Faithfulness

When God gives a talent, He never takes it back. Romans 11:29 says, "For the gifts and calling of God are without repentance." "Repentance" here means God won't change His mind. However, the opportunity to *use* the gifts and fulfill the callings of God may pass away with time.

What if we misuse a gift? If we repent humbly, God will help us, but He still will hold us accountable for the gift. Notice the verse also says the *calling* of God — His invitation to use the gift — is such that God won't change His mind. Paul realized that his brethren would sometimes neglect their gifts. So he instructed Timothy to "stir up the gift of God, which is in thee by the putting on of my hands" (2 Tim. 1:6) and to "neglect not the gift that is in thee" (1 Tim. 4:14).

We should do with our lives whatever our talents and gifts indicate we should do. But it should be done for the glory of God, in trust.

First Corinthians 4:1-2 says, "Let a man so account of us, as of the ministers of Christ, and stewards of the mysteries of God. Moreover it is required in stewards, that a man be found faithful."

It doesn't say he shall be found a genius. It doesn't say he shall be well-educated, though that may help some to be better stewards. But God does require one thing: faithfulness. At the judgment may we confidently expect to hear, "Well done, thou good and faithful servant. Enter thou into the joy of thy Lord" (see Matt. 25:21).

And after that judgment, the truly exciting rewards of stewardship will begin. As the next chapter will show, God has prepared eternal realms of stewardship for us beyond what we can now imagine.

TWENTY

PREPARING
TO REIGN

The law of God's
intended destiny for man

G autama Siddhartha, a young nobleman from India, decided to devote himself to trying to unveil the mystery of life. He became the founder of Buddhism.

His efforts brought him to one basic conclusion: All of life's troubles come from things we want and cannot always have. He reasoned that we could reduce pain by reducing our desires. If an individual has practically no desires, he would (in theory) have practically no pain. When life is over, if a person could be absorbed into nothingness, life could be absorbed into a state of painlessness.

What a sterile view of life! What is the purpose of going through earthly challenge and suffering? If you are merely a lone cog in such a mighty but aimless machine, how can you find satisfaction in that? Something within every person struggles against the idea of life without meaning.

Many people still subscribe to the philosophy of the ancient Epicureans, who said, "That is good which causes you joy. If virtue causes joy, then be virtuous. If pleasure causes joy, then follow pleasure."

The Epicureans, however, could only plead ignorance when asked what happens after death. They guessed that souls would be absorbed into a great river of life. This is another form of Buddhism — the belief that your person-hood will cease. But there is a dynamic part of you that says, No! I am a person, and I am important.

A commercial for hair conditioner features a woman who says, "It costs a little more, *but I'm worth it.*" That's true! Something in life makes you and me worth something.

In the apostle Paul's day, the Stoics had a somewhat noble philosophy: Virtue is its own reward. Virtue is good because in the long run it is better to be virtuous than to be evil or selfish. But the only profit they could see in this was a happier life. The Stoics, like the Epicureans, had nothing to offer for what happens after death. They could only say, "We suppose we are like the candle that is extinguished. Where does the light go? Out! So it is with man."

All such worldly philosophies come to a dead end. They don't know what to do beyond death. But is there another answer for you and me?

As Christians, we know there is — eternal life with Christ. But did you know there is more than just an open-ended invitation to heaven? The fullness of our afterlife is revealed in the law of God's intended destiny for man: *God is training us as stewards to rule with Him over His creation.*

Financial Stewardship

Snuffed candles and anonymous drops in the river of life do not figure in God's plan for His people. Jesus said, "In my Father's house are many mansions: if it were not so, I would have told you. I go to prepare a place for you. And if I go and prepare a place for you, I will come again, and receive you unto myself; that where I am, there ye may be also" (John 14:2-3).

As we prepare for entering those mansions, God has laid out for us glorious opportunities to serve Him. He delights in our service, because as children of God we are automatically members of His royal household. You may not feel like it, but you are royalty!

Since you are important to God, what does He intend to do with you? Here are several doctrines of Christ which tell us in just a few words something of the beautiful, exciting future God makes available to you.

"And the Lord said, Who then is that faithful and wise steward?" (Luke 12:42). A steward is a person who operates something on behalf of its owner.

We often speak of tithing as stewardship, because giving a tenth is God's way of supporting His work and proving to each of us that we are in fact stewards. By giving one-tenth of our increase (or income) to God's work in the church, we demonstrate that all we have belongs to God and stands ready for use at His command.

Are you a steward? Do you regard everything you have, not only your money, but all your talent, your time and your possessions as a trust from God? Do you know that He wants you to make Him Lord over all so He can acknowledge you are a steward? It is easy to speak generally, saying, "I am the servant of God." But if we have truly adopted a heart of servanthood, we must be able to say, "I am the steward of God."

Of course, our Father is the most generous and practical

of lords. He will tell you to take some of His money and pay taxes; Jesus did that. He will tell you to take some of His money and enjoy a vacation; Jesus did that. He will tell you to take some of His money to feed and clothe yourself and your family. And He will tell you to take some of His money and save it. What matters is that from the beginning to the end of your decision-making process, you acknowledge that what you earn is God's and that you desire nothing more than to be a good steward over God's wealth.

An Eye to Eternity

Stewardship of time is just as important as stewardship of money. Perhaps you have never tithed your time and your service unto God, but that is also part of what we are talking about. If you are to be more than a drop of water absorbed into the river of life, if you are to be an individual, then what on earth are you going to do?

Be a servant! That assignment doesn't end with this life. You are being trained here for eternity — *to rule God's universe with Him*. Second Timothy 2:12 promises, "We shall also reign with him."

That is why God entrusts you with His kingdom here, at least a little part of it — with your gifts and skills, with money, time and opportunity. He says, "I'm going to see how you use it. Then I'll determine where I'm going to put you as My servant and a member of the royal family, a prince or a princess in eternity."

In Luke 12:42 — "Who then is that faithful and wise steward, whom his lord shall make ruler over his household...?" — Jesus is talking not just about ordinary homes, but about the local church as the household of God. He has placed His servants, His children, as members of the royal family, in training over smaller matters that they may be placed as faithful stewards over the church.

"Blessed is that servant, whom his lord when he cometh

shall find so doing. Of a truth I say unto you, that he will make him ruler over all that he hath" (Luke 12:43-44). What is "all that God hath"? He has the whole earth. He has the whole solar system. He has this universe and, if they exist, other universes. "The earth is the Lord's, and the fullness thereof" (Ps. 24:1).

Not only are we to live forever, but we are to live creatively, dynamically and responsibly. How dare we live cheap, small lives! We spend hours focusing on scratched auto fenders and petty office disputes, ignoring that God has given us this life that we might become faithful and wise stewards. Let us not lose sight of the reality that He wants to share with us the rulership of all that He has.

God's Call on Your Life

How do we find the optimum place of service that God wants us to render?

Consider the young church in Acts 13. When ministry work in the large city of Antioch got so heavy that Barnabas needed a helper, he sent for Paul, who was fifty miles away at Tarsus. When he and Barnabas finally began to work together, their chemistry made them so effective they had a church boom on their hands.

> As they ministered to the Lord, and fasted, the Holy Ghost said, Separate me Barnabas and Saul for the work whereunto I have called them. And when they had fasted and prayed, and laid their hands on them, they sent them away. So they, being sent forth by the Holy Ghost, departed unto Seleucia (Acts 13:2-4).

It was the Holy Spirit who set Paul and Barnabas aside for the work God called them to do. In the same way, your service must not be done through self-will, but as the Holy

Spirit directs. The Spirit desires to put us into whatever classes or service will best train us for that which will last forever. Embrace whatever troubles or challenges you face today, because they are part of your training for tomorrow.

Look at life as a kind of West Point or Annapolis. A student in these schools learns how to obey commands, how to take assignments and responsibilities. Only upon graduation is the student assigned to a command. If the young officer is successful, he gets promoted to a higher command. When God gives you a small task to do, and you are faithful, He gives you more responsibility.

Acts 13:2 refers to a ministry "called" forth by God. While I believe in a "called" ministry, I also believe a greater truth: that the "ministry" includes everybody in the church. God calls some to teach the Word, some to preach it, some to do other things. But He calls us all! You're no less precious as a servant in God's sight than a minister on the church staff. You are created in the image of God, who wants you in His training school to prepare you for high command.

Gifts for All

You might think, What if God calls me to do something I can't do? Worry not. The manifestation of the gifts that God gives through the Holy Spirit is available to *every man!* If God calls us, He equips us for the task. He is not stingy with His giftings.

As Paul wrote, "Now there are diversities of gifts, but the same Spirit. And there are differences of administrations, but the same Lord. And there are diversities of operations, but it is the same God which worketh all in all. But the manifestation of the Spirit is given to every man to profit withal" (1 Cor. 12:4).

Maybe you believe you can't find your proper role of spiritual service. Or maybe you've found it, but feel that nobody wants you or has any use for you. Don't believe it!

Paul explained that the body of Christ is composed of many members, which mysteriously form only one body:

> And the eye cannot say unto the hand, I have no need of thee: nor again the head to the feet, I have no need of you. Nay, much more those members of the body, which seem to be more feeble, are necessary: And those members of the body, which we think to be less honourable, upon these we bestow more abundant honour; and our uncomely parts have more abundant comeliness (1 Cor. 12:21-23).

Once you discern your gifting from God, do not despise it. He had you in mind when He granted it, and He has big plans for you. Remember, you are made in His image to rule over all He has. But this will not come about apart from your stewardship over the gifts of the Holy Spirit and your faithfulness to the Spirit's continual leading. Pray that God will make this high calling become real in your life now.

TWENTY-ONE

MIND YOUR MIND

The law of transformation

More people suffer from arthritis of the mind than from arthritis of the bones. If that's the case, you might wonder, why is it that aging people gripe so much about their aching hands or shoulders? The difference is that people with stiffening minds, while they may have no shortage of complaints, don't realize the real source of their problems.

Would you believe that some people have escaped many of the common handicaps of old age, such as boredom, worry, loneliness, forgetfulness? Those who nearly defy the aging process almost always have one thing in common: *They keep their minds alive.*

We should fight with every ounce of our being against the temptation to become set in our ways. We need to be creative, to keep mentally active and continue greeting each day as an opportunity to be something more than we were yesterday. The moment we stop growing and learning, the moment our minds become inflexible, the penalties of age set in. It is not necessary. But like every other organ of the body, the mind starts to settle like concrete unless it is deliberately exercised.

Shaping the Mind

Nobody really knows what the mind is. The Greek word we translate as "mind" has three translations — intellect, feeling and will. It involves the totality of the personality, that which makes us who we are.

But more to the point, *the mind, as the seat of our thoughts, is vitally important to our success.* Proverbs 23:7 exhorts, "For as he thinketh in his heart, so is he." Romans 12:2 encourages healthy thinking: "And be not conformed to this world: but be ye transformed by the renewing of your mind, that ye may prove what is that good, and acceptable, and perfect, will of God."

In other words, don't let this world's standards shape you. Dismiss the world, its claims, pressures and attractions. You've been delivered from that. Herein lies the clue to resisting that hardening of the mental muscles: *We avoid mental ruts by being transformed in our minds.*

Avoiding worldly conformity does not mean becoming a religious conformist. Many people think Christians are cross-bearing drones — with long faces and behavior rooted in a list of "thou shalt nots." Unfortunately, the observation has some validity to it.

Yet nowhere does the Bible teach that. There are certain

things we are not to do, but the Bible — especially the New Testament — is far more interested in what we are supposed to be and do rather than what we're *not* supposed to do. Jesus was not alluding to a life based on no-nos when He said, "I am come that they might have life, and that they might have it more abundantly" (John 10:10).

Now that we know what not to be conformed to — the world and empty religion — what then? Be transformed. Christ has given us the privilege of living a transformed life. This process begins at conversion and continues throughout life. The further we walk with Jesus, the less we conform to this world and the more we are transformed into His likeness. This, then, is the law of transformation: *We are transformed into being like Christ by the renewing of our minds.*

This is not a mental renewal precipitated by education or popular philosophies. Many Christians are not even aware that what passes for the gospel in their church is nothing more than baptized psychology. Newspaper church advertisements announce catchy sermon topics that contain no more gospel than a garbage can.

The Greek word for "renewing" is akin to the word "springtime." It is only because of the power of the living seed Christ plants within us that we can enjoy a continuous springtime, the coming of new life, the bursting of the buds, the freshening of the rains, the shooting forth of the green shoots. We can, and we should, experience this constant renewing of the mind. Other sources may counterfeit this renewal temporarily, but only Christ holds the key to the eternal spring of water that runs ever new.

The Bible helps us discern different kinds of minds, or more accurately, different attitudes of the mind. I have found seven different categories, representing seven different approaches to life. Three of them are bad; one is neutral; and three are good.

Let's examine first the bad side to see what characteristics of the mind need to be renewed.

Blind Minds

> But their minds were blinded: for until this day remaineth the same veil untaken away in the reading of the old testament; which veil is done away in Christ. But even unto this day, when Moses is read, the veil is upon their heart (2 Cor. 3:14-15).

The Scripture passage refers to blinded minds. Jesus said such people are willingly ignorant, spiritually blinded.

Christians frequently encounter blinded minds when they are witnessing. No argument, no testimony, no imparting of the truth can get through.

That's because most people have difficulty when it comes to facing the truth about themselves and God. I've lost friends and alienated other people by telling them the truth.

The Jews are another example. Not only in Christ's day was there a veil over the Old Testament as well as their hearts, but over the centuries many of them have been blinded to the messianic role of Jesus.

The Reprobate Mind

> And even as they did not like to retain God in their knowledge, God gave them over to a reprobate mind, to do those things which are not convenient (Rom. 1:28).

"Reprobate" refers to a person with a reputation for committing corrupt acts, someone who is absorbed in evil, with a degenerate mind. Romans 1 continues with the most complete list of gross sins to be catalogued in the Bible, the fruit of a reprobate mind:

> Being filled with all unrighteousness, fornication, wickedness, covetousness, maliciousness; full of

envy, murder, debate, malignity; whisperers, backbiters, haters of God, despiteful, proud, boasters, inventors of evil things, disobedient to parents, without understanding, covenant breakers, without natural affection, implacable, unmerciful (Rom. 1:29-31).

The Carnal Mind

For they that are after the flesh do mind the things of the flesh; but they that are after the Spirit the things of the Spirit. For to be carnally minded is death; but to be spiritually minded is life and peace. Because the carnal mind is enmity against God: for it is not subject to the law of God, neither indeed can be (Rom. 8:5).

This word "carnal" is well-known to most Christians. It involves the appetites of the flesh — such as gluttony, illicit sex and envy. But it is not limited to those obviously carnal cravings. People who allow hobbies, for example, to dominate their time and thought-life at the expense of spiritual things are carnally minded.

These are the three basic kinds of evil mind-sets portrayed in Scripture: blind, reprobate and carnal. The fourth kind is not necessarily good or bad, but it can easily lead one into spiritual problems.

The Weary Mind

For consider him that endured such contradiction of sinners against himself, lest ye be wearied and faint in your minds (Heb. 12:3).

Christians can encounter the weary or faint mind, especially when they neglect their spiritual nutrition, fail to read the Word of God, become lazy in their prayer lives, avoid fellowship with God's people and refuse to take responsibility in the kingdom of God or in the church. Their faith can grow weak and their courage faint, until they just don't feel like doing anything.

I've met scores of people who say, "I just don't have the interest in Christ I used to have. The fires on the altar of my heart have grown dim, though the coals are still there. I still hope for Jesus; I still believe in the church; I still love the Bible, but I've grown weak."

This state of mind is more dangerous than it is evil. The danger, of course, is that unresolved stagnation is fatal, whether it's physical or spiritual. Christians not growing in Christ tend to be falling away from Him.

The Pure Mind

This second epistle, beloved, I now write unto you; in both which I stir up your pure minds by way of remembrance (2 Pet. 3:1).

Though all of us are sinners and occasionally manifest bad kinds of mind, we have the ability to possess a pure mind, because the Author of purity lives within us. What does Peter recommend? Stir up your minds by reviewing the great doctrines of the faith, the Person and work of Jesus, and the believer's responsibilities and privileges.

The Mind to Work

So built we the wall [of Jerusalem]; and all the wall was joined together unto the half thereof: for the people had a mind to work (Neh. 4:6).

How quickly things get done when people have a mind to work!

190

Remember the parable of the man who buried his talent (a piece of money)? This displeased God, who took the talent from him and gave it to a man with ten talents. God wants people who bring results. God wants people who grow and progress. God desires us to prove that we can double the talents He has entrusted to us. If we don't, what excuse will we give Him when we stand before Him at life's end?

The Lowly Mind

Let nothing be done through strife or vainglory; but in lowliness of mind let each esteem other better than themselves. Look not every man on his own things, but every man also on the things of others. Let this mind be in you, which was also in Christ Jesus: who, being in the form of God, thought it not robbery to be equal with God: but made himself of no reputation, and took upon him the form of a servant, and was made in the likeness of men: and being found in fashion as a man, he humbled himself, and became obedient unto death, even the death of the cross. Wherefore God also hath highly exalted him, and given him a name which is above every name (Phil. 2:3-9).

Paul exhorts us to resist things such as jealousy over our reputation. We must not be always looking after our own interests alone. To look after the affairs of others, to be concerned about their feelings and welfare, is the injunction. In short, be like Jesus. Let this mind which was in Christ Jesus be also in you.

The mind of Christ is holy, pure, redemptive and merciful. But it has one quality that Paul speaks about here more than any other: humility. A double-minded man is unstable in all his ways, but a humble-minded person, whose thoughts are focused singly on Christ, begins to think like Christ. He has found the secret of happiness.

Your Choice

Thus we can have any of the seven minds described by Scripture. We did not simply inherit one at birth. Rather it is our choice as to which kind we will have, whether we will choose from the three categories of good minds. Only by doing so can we experience the ongoing renewal of our minds promised by Scripture. We will see next that this transformation affects not just our minds, but our whole being.

TWENTY-TWO

DESTINED FOR A NEW IMAGE

The law of God's eternal purpose for the believer

In the 1600s Galileo pushed back the frontiers of the universe by his proof that Copernicus was right: The earth is not the focal point of our solar system; the planets revolve around the sun.

One of the unfortunate side effects of his astounding revelation was a diminished perspective on the importance of man. Secular scientists eventually declared that man is the result of a molecular accident that produced simple life, gradually evolving into *homo sapiens*. Consequently, man has been increasingly lost in the vastness of an impersonal universe, snared in an eternal cycle of meaningless living and dying, totally bereft of meaning or purpose.

Against this backdrop of darkness, Christianity stands out like a beacon of hope, proclaiming that there is indeed a purpose to life, that we can and must discover that purpose and adjust our lives to its imperatives. One cannot enjoy complete mental and emotional health otherwise. Carl Jung, the famous Swiss psychiatrist, wrote that he had dealt with few, if any, cases in which the root problem was not somehow connected to the lack of religious certainty. That uncertainty is another way of saying a lack of divine purpose for one's life.

Unchanging Purpose

The Bible, by contrast, brims over with divine purpose. The first hint of it comes in the first chapter: "And God said, Let us make man in our own image, after our likeness" (Gen. 1:26).

God wastes no time in revealing that attaining His likeness is a part of our reason for living. It is evident from this and other biblical passages, such as Genesis 9:11 and Acts 17:29, that man *should* bear the image of God. It's also obvious, of course, that man has fallen short of that goal. He more often resembles the demonic than the divine.

What is actually presented in the New Testament is that we be conformed to the image of Jesus rather than that of the Father. Jesus is "the brightness of his [God's] glory, and the express image of his person" (Heb. 1:3). That is, Jesus is the exact reflection of God. The phrase "express image" comes from the Greek *karakter*, from which we get "character." *Karakter* means a stamped or impressed image, directly resembling the original. Jesus, as the Son of God, is therefore the truest image of God that one can find. Thus, as we strive to attain the image of Jesus, we will begin to resemble God.

This is the purpose of man's existence, as spelled out in

Romans 8:29: "For whom he did foreknow, he also did predestinate to be conformed to the image of his Son."

With this we are brought back to the eternal calling mentioned in Hebrews and Genesis — the law of God's eternal purpose for the believer: *God intends that His children be conformed to the image of His Son.*

This same truth is repeated throughout the New Testament:

"As we have borne the image of the earthy, we shall also bear the image of the heavenly" (1 Cor. 15:49).

"According to the eternal purpose which he purposed in Christ Jesus our Lord" (Eph. 3:11).

Jesus "shall change our vile body, that it may be fashioned like unto his glorious body" (Phil. 3:21).

"Beloved, now are we the sons of God, and it doth not yet appear what we shall be: but we know that, when he shall appear, we shall be like him; for we shall see him as he is" (1 John 3:2).

The destiny of man is not to please his Maker through good works or a renowned ministry. It is simply to be conformed into the image of Christ. This highest of callings is available to every Christian.

Sooner or Later

How many of us have really stopped to ponder the implications of this need to become more like Christ? The *pièce de résistance* of the law of God's eternal purpose for the believer is not only that Christians ought to be like Jesus, but that we are going to be like Him, whether we intend it or not.

Recall that Romans 8:29 says God predestined those He foreknew "to be conformed to the image of his Son." Forgetting all theological wrangling as to predestination, free will and salvation, this fact cannot be escaped: When God predestines a thing, it always comes to pass. Therefore *we shall be* conformed to the image of Christ, because Scripture promises it.

A person is still free to choose whether or not to accept Christ. But once the choice to follow Christ is made, the die is cast forever. After we are born again into God's family, we become children of God, and our Father immediately assumes the task of disciplining us into conformity to Christ's image. He may encounter stubbornness and rebellion; consequently, most people will require a continuation of the process after their life on earth. But count on it: God always does what He sets out to do.

Jesus was asked by a rich young ruler of the Jews what a man must do to be saved. Jesus answered that he must sell all that he had, give the proceeds to the poor, take up his cross and follow Him. Jesus, in essence, was asking the young man to be conformed to His image. How so? Jesus forsook all that He had; He gave to the poor; though He was rich, for our sakes He became poor; and He would some day take up His cross. But when the young man saw all that was involved, he was unwilling to do it. He turned and left in sorrow.

In order that every Christian be Christlike, the death of much of what we call self will have to be involved. Dying to our own desires and instead doing only those things which please the Lord is a painful process, but this is our goal, and reach it we shall.

The question is, will we begin *now* to reflect that image in our daily walk with Christ? Will we begin to work immediately at the task of becoming as much like Jesus as we can and in the shortest possible time?

From Glory to Glory

But we all, with open face beholding as in a glass the glory of the Lord, are changed into the same image from glory to glory, even as by the Spirit of the Lord (2 Cor. 3:18).

The transformation into Christlikeness is another way of describing complete submission to the will of the Father. It takes place gradually, from glory to glory.

A classic illustration of this eternal truth is found in Ralph Waldo Emerson's story "The Great Stone Face." A village legend foretold of a day when a great man would arrive. He would personify many virtues and would resemble the image of a man's face visible in the stony outcropping on the cliffside overlooking this hamlet.

Ernest, a village lad, gazed each day upon the noble image in the cliffs. As the years passed, several great men were hailed as the ones who fulfilled the prophecy; yet none of them actually did. In the meantime Ernest went on living a simple, virtuous life, continuing to look at the rock, hoping to see his ideals fulfilled. He expected confidently to welcome some day the man who would resemble the stone face.

As he came to the sunset of life, the villagers suddenly realized that Ernest himself had been slowly transformed by his ideals into the very likeness of that great stone face and all it embodied. He became the fulfillment of the prophecy that had been his magnificent obsession.

That is, of course, only a partial truth, because those who do not know Christ but strive to be accepted by God through good works in the name of Christianity will be greatly disappointed. So will those who admire Jesus as a great role model — who gaze upon His greatness, as Ernest might have done — but fail to submit to His lordship, to die to self and live to Christ.

But like this story, the Christian looks into the face of Christ, and despite the infirmities of his life, he is gradually transformed into that glorious image. Like Ernest, he will be pleasantly surprised, because the lofty visage of Christ seems so unattainable, so transcendent — yet it is our destiny. Looming above our ambitions, our possessions, our pleasures, our pursuits, is this overmastering purpose God has for us.

Each day we should be able to see in ourselves — and others should see it too — a growth toward a fuller realization of God's divine purpose to transform us into the image of Christ. Every act, every decision, should be made in the light of whether it contributes to this ultimate purpose. Our character growth can be measured only by whether or not we grow *toward* Christlikeness.

What reward is in this occasionally painful process? Will we have to give up all our fun? Is it really worth doing?

We will not have to forsake all pleasure, though the Bible warns we shouldn't be surprised if suffering comes our way. Suffering for the sake of Christ is nothing to shun. In fact, it plays a part in God's purpose for creating the human race, which is to bring His children into glory — that is, the reflection of His Son.

"For it became him, for whom are all things, and by whom are all things, in bringing many sons unto glory, to make the captain of their salvation perfect through sufferings" (Heb. 2:10). "If we suffer, we shall also reign with him: if we deny him, he also will deny us" (2 Tim. 2:12). Though being transformed into the image of Christ may entail suffering, and though it certainly will mean death to self and the surrender of our stubborn wills to His divine will, it *is* worth it.

We can appreciate that worth if we come to view the transformation process in terms of long-range rewards. Psalm 16:11 assures us, "Thou wilt show me the path of life: in thy presence is fulness of joy; at thy right hand there are pleasures for evermore." To inhabit eternity with God, conformed to the image of His Son, is to be in actuality God's child. The Son of God, Jesus, resembles the Father, and so too we are going to resemble Jesus. We are going to bear the imprint of Christ, conformed to His character.

Imagine it: a son of God! Only those who are finally

conformed to the image of His Son are fit to inhabit eternity with a perfect God.

The question is, can we open our hearts and yearn toward Christlikeness? Can we begin now, or must our stubborn wills delay the process? Can we forsake our sins and ask forgiveness for them? That is exactly what He will do if we will say, "O God, forgive me for ugly behavior; forgive me for displays of temper; forgive me for envy, for jealousy, for lust, for shutting You out. O God, help me to be conformed to the image of Your dear Son so that all the love You have poured out on Jesus may also be poured out upon me."

With that attitude, God will be faithful to mold us into a new likeness. As He does, as the final chapter shows, we will find ourselves attaining the fullness of maturity in Christ.

TWENTY-THREE

GROW UP!

The law of finding your true goal in life

I was browsing about in the shops of Bangkok, Thailand, when I ventured inside a big corner shop. I was not prepared for what I found.

There were idols all about, each with its price tag. Most were made of plaster, gilded with gold or enamel paint. Some of them stood ten feet tall. These were not merely souvenirs for visitors such as I, but statues intended to be worshipped. *I have never felt the presence of Satan more acutely than I felt it at that moment.* It was not just the images themselves, but the satanic power that lies behind them.

We Americans hear about idol worship. We read about it in the Bible. We know that a great share of the undeveloped world still worships idols.

As alien as these images may seem to our modern, cultured minds, as shocking as this room full of consumer gods appeared to me in Thailand, they touch on the root of something that is universal and never goes out of practice. I refer to the law of finding your true goal in life: *The ideal for every Christian is Christian maturity, which is putting God first in all things.*

Scripture's Final Word

This law comes into focus when you take a close look at the profound first letter of John, which the apostle wrote when he was over ninety years old. In actions and attitudes he was venerable, like a father. His favorite term of address to his flock was "little children" (in Christ).

While the elaborate book of Revelation, also written by John, is located at the very end of the Bible, it may have been written before the starkly simple 1 John. Second John and 3 John also may have been written prior to 1 John, meaning these may have been the last words of Scripture he would write.

The epistle does not address baptism, conversion or regular church doctrine. It does not lay Christian foundations, as do the Gospels and the books of Romans and Acts.

Rather 1 John is a climax to all of God's revelation. In that sense, regardless of when it was produced, it is the epistle of maturity. It is the final word, those matters which needed to be written before the full revelation of God to man would be finished.

Following a passage about how Jesus has come to impart true understanding, John changes the subject for an abrupt conclusion: "Little children, keep yourselves from idols. Amen" (1 John 5:21).

Having gone to such depths in writing to Christians in need of instructions for growth and maturity, why would John suddenly look outside Christianity and wag his finger over idol worship? The advice seems out of place.

Yet nothing that the Bible has for us is more important. I am convinced this exhortation was intended by the Holy Spirit to be the final word of Scripture. Why? *Because there is an unrecognized tendency in all of us to worship idols.*

You might object, "We may have committed many sins, but we have never worshipped an idol." But that is the whole point: Christians today do not fully understand idol worship. In America it's not easy to find an idol in the common sense of the word. You could possibly locate them in Chinatown or maybe in the Japanese section of a large city, but most Americans have never seen, much less worshipped, something on the order of the golden statues I saw in Thailand.

Another thing Americans often misunderstand is that when people worship idols they are not necessarily rejecting the idea of God. They are substituting a false god for the true God. The devotees may be deluded into worshipping Satan or a demon, but they are still *worshipping*. No atheist ever worships anything, even an idol. This is not to add any justification to idol worship, but just to show how easily even Christians can be drawn into idol worship though they have never renounced Christ.

Our Kind of Idolatry

We do not bow down before a statue of Buddha and pray to it every day. We don't worship Kali, the Indian goddess with sixteen arms. What we do, though, is exactly what the idol worshippers do: *We substitute other things for God.* "Worship" means "worthship," the concept that whatever you hold in highest worth is actually your god.

How easy it is to allow the demands of a job to consume

more and more of your time. It's hard to resist the temptation to allocate to your work the time you could be spending in church services or ministry. And the lure of earning ever greater amounts of money is more than some people are able to control. Whenever you put your business ahead of God, it has become your idol.

In some of the ministries at church, you may attend as long as you don't have some other social engagement. But when that other attraction comes along, it is first. Instead of bringing your friends and relatives to God's house and sharing the joy of Christ, you surrender to them. This means you have exalted certain people over God, making them, or their approval of you, an idol.

Do you really have the joy of Christ? You can't if God isn't first in your life. It is nice to sing about "peace on earth, good will toward men" and how we hate war. But the real heart of peace is not how man defines it, but the surrender of your life to God, putting Him first.

When you and I stand before the believer's judgment, the paramount question will be, Whom did you place first? We will be judged according to how we measured up to Jesus' command: "Seek ye first the kingdom of God, and his righteousness; and all these things shall be added unto you" (Matt. 6:33). If you have the courage to put Him first, He will reward you a thousand times more than whatever you are tempted to value ahead of Him.

Christian maturity — putting God first in all things — is the ideal for every Christian, not just preachers. There is no hindrance to your spiritual upward mobility. How I rejoice in that!

So it is that Paul wrote, "But we all, with open face beholding as in a glass the glory of the Lord, are changed into the same image from glory to glory, even as by the Spirit of the Lord" (2 Cor. 3:18). We're to fix our gaze on the glory of the Lord. If you've got your eye on the preacher, please change channels. At best, he is one who is constantly in training, trying to learn fresh things from the Word of God and present them to you in a way that will reach your life. Place your eyes on Christ, the head of the church, and let the Spirit change you to be like Him.

Carnal Christians, the Bible says, divide into factions. Paul rebuked the Corinthian Christians for saying, "I am of Paul; and I of Apollos; and I of Cephas" (1 Cor. 1:12). He was essentially pointing out idolatry. By placing teachers ahead of Christ, they were short-circuiting the path of Christian maturity.

Veils That Obscure Jesus

When Paul instructed the Corinthians to gaze upon the Lord with open — that is, unveiled — faces, he was not writing about the social practice of veiling the faces of women. He was talking about how when Moses came down from the mountain after seeing God, the people who looked upon his face were blinded. Therefore he put a veil over his face.

Paul used that illustration to show that God's will has been, in a sense, *veiled* for the Jews. If the Jews really understood God's will, they would come to Christ. But Paul said Christians can look upon Jesus with unveiled faces, beholding His glory.

What are some other "veils" that hinder us from fixing our gaze upon Jesus? First, the veil of blaming other people or our circumstances for our sins. How easy it is to blame our parents, our childhood, our teachers or the neighborhood in which we grew up. How convenient for young people to cite peer pressure as the reason they caved in to temptations for drugs, alcohol or sex. The swiftest route into Christian maturity is to accept responsibility for what you are. As an old hymn says, "It's not my father, not my mother, but it's me, O Lord, standing in the need of prayer."

Or you may say, "I've tried praying; God doesn't hear

me." You get drawn within yourself. Your view of Christ has been clouded by your doubt of being accepted by God.

Other veils are discouragement, defeatism, self-love, envy, jealousy, self-centeredness, bad habits, bad friendships, feelings of inferiority, even guilt. All can veil the glory of God. We've got to get rid of them, putting them under the blood of Christ, saying, "Lord, I won't have those things hindering me from seeing You."

You probably have some veil today obscuring the glory of God. You've just been separated from your husband, and you're bitter? Give it up to God. You've just been widowed, and you're blaming God? Give it up. Are you envious? Jealous? Full of unforgiveness? Give these things up to God!

No wonder people buy so much Alka Seltzer: "Plop, plop, fizz, fizz, oh, what a relief it is!" The whole nation is bubbling with resentments and looking for a quick fix. How much better to get a fix that will last by surrendering all to Christ.

Let us begin now by laying aside every weight and the sin that so easily besets us. Drop the veil so you can see God in His glory and have nothing standing between you and Christ! You will be transformed into the image of Christ as you behold His face, as you lay aside the veils!

Obey Him. Accept responsibility for His assembly, the church. Put Him first. Love His commandments and obey them. Christian maturity, the goal God intends for you to achieve, will be yours!

A national correspondence school advertised, "How many decisive years do you have left?" You too would do well to ask yourself how many decisive years you still have. How many years when you can change your view of Christ, seeing Him as preeminent, so that you can be used fully by Him to extend His kingdom? Perhaps not many. Then decide now that you will do the will of God every minute from now on. Your role in eternity depends upon your faithfulness here. Do not delay embracing it!

BIBLIOGRAPHY

The following are useful books on the kingdom of God:

Alves, Colin. *The Kingdom.* Cambridge, England: University Press, 1959.

Arlington, Cyril Argentine. *The Kingdom of God.* London: The Centenary Press, 1940.

Baughman, Ray E. *The Kingdom of God Visualized.* Chicago: Moody Press, 1972.

Berkhof, Louis. *The Kingdom of God.* Grand Rapids, Mich.: Wm. B. Eerdmans Publishing Co., 1951.

Boardman, George Dana. *The Kingdom of God.* New York: C. Scribner's Sons, 1899.

Bright, John. *The Kingdom of God.* Nashville, Tenn.: Abingdon Press, 1953.

Bruce, Alexander B. *The Kingdom of God.* Edinburgh: T. & T. Clark; New York: C. Scribner's Sons, 1891.

Candlish, James Stuart. *The Kingdom of God.* Edinburgh: T. & T. Clark, 1884.

Carnell, Edward J. *Kingdom of Love and the Pride of Life.* Grand Rapids, Mich.: Wm. B. Eerdmans Publishing Co., 1960.

Chilton, Bruce (editor). *The Kingdom of God in the Teaching of Jesus.* Philadelphia: Fortress Press; London: SPCK, 1984.

Danker, Frederick W. *The Kingdom in Action.* St. Louis: Concordia Publishing House, 1965.

Evans, Louis Hadley. *The Kingdom Is Yours.* New Jersey: Fleming H. Revell, 1952.

Hamilton, E.L. *The Laws and Principles of the Kingdom of Heaven.* London: Marshall Bros., Ltd.

Harris, Samuel. *The Kingdom of Christ on Earth*. Andover: Warren F. Draper, 1874.

Herrick, Henry M. *The Kingdom of God in the Writings of the Fathers*. Chicago: University of Chicago Press, 1903.

Hiers, Richard H. *The Kingdom of God in the Synoptic Tradition*. Gainesville: University of Florida Press, 1970.

Hooke, Samuel H. *The Kingdom of God in the Experience of Jesus*. London: Gerald Duckworth & Co., 1949.

Hughes, H. Maldwyn. *The Kingdom of Heaven*. London: The Epworth Press, 1922.

Jones, E. Stanley. *The Unshakable Kingdom and the Unchanging Person*. Nashville, New York: Abingdon Press, 1972.

Karrer, Otto. *The Kingdom of God Today*. Ockenden: Freiburg, Herder, 1964.

Kelber, Werner H. *The Kingdom in Mark*. Philadelphia: Fortress Press, 1974.

Ladd, George E. *The Gospel of the Kingdom*. Grand Rapids, Mich.: Wm. B. Eerdmans Publishing Co., 1961.

Ladd, George E. *Crucial Questions About the Kingdom of God*. Grand Rapids, Mich.: Wm. B. Eerdmans Publishing Co., 1954.

Lundstrom, Gosta. *The Kingdom of God in the Teaching of Jesus*. Edinburgh: Oliver and Boyd, 1963.

Macinnes, Alexander M.F. *The Kingdom of God in the Apostolic Writings*. London: J. Clarke & Co., Ltd., 1924.

MacLaren, Alexander. *A Garland of Gladness*. Grand Rapids, Mich.: Wm. B. Eerdmans Publishing Co., 1945.

Maurice, Frederick D. *The Kingdom of Christ*. London: Macmillan, 1891.

Minear, Paul Sevier. *The Kingdom and the Power*. Philadelphia: Westminster Press, 1950.

Otto, Rudolf. *The Kingdom of God and the Son of Man*. London: Lutterworth Press, 1938.

Paul, Robert S. *Kingdom Come!* Grand Rapids, Mich.: Wm. B. Eerdmans Publishing Co., 1974.

Perrin, Norman. *The Kingdom of God in the Teaching of Jesus*.

London: SCM Press, 1963.

Riggle, H.M. *The Kingdom of God*. Guthrie, Okla.: Faith Publishing House, 1899.

Rinne, W. *The Kingdom in the Thought of William Temple*. Abo, Abo Akademi, 1966.

Ross, J.J. *The Kingdom in Mystery*. Chicago: Fleming H. Revell, 1920.

Schweitzer, Albert. *The Kingdom of God and Primitive Christianity*. London: Black, 1968.

Scott, Ernest Findlay. *The Kingdom and the Messiah*. Edinburgh: T. & T. Clark, 1911.

Scott, Ernest Findlay. *The Kingdom of God in the New Testament*. New York: The Macmillan Co., 1931.

Sharman, Henry B. *Son of Man, and Kingdom of God*. New York: Harper & Bros., 1943.